CREATED BY
CLAUDIO SANCHEZ

WRITTEN BY
CLAUDIO SANCHEZ AND CHONDRA ECHERT

ART, LETTERS, AND COVER BY
MR. SHELDON

ART ASSISTS BY
NIKI LOPEZ
ZAC ATKINSON
ALUISIO CERVELLE SANTOS

EVIL INK COMICS

IAN BRILL EDITOR, HARDCOVER EDITION
BRYCE CARLSON EDITOR, SOFTCOVER EDITION
ADAM STAFFARONI ASSISTANT EDITOR, SOFTCOVER EDITION
BRIAN LATIMER GRAPHIC DESIGNER, HARDCOVER EDITION
CAROL THOMPSON GRAPHIC DESIGNER, SOFTCOVER EDITION

For information regarding the CPSIA on this printed material, call: (203) 595-3636 and provide reference #RICH – 437368. A catalog record of this book is available from OCLC and from the BOOM! Studios website, www.boom-studios.com, on the Librarians Page.

BOOM! Studios, 6310 San Vicente Boulevard, Suite 107, Los Angeles, CA 90048-5457. Printed in USA. First Printing, Trade Paperback. ISBN: 978-1-60886-292-4

TIME TO FACE THE MUSIC

TO FIND THE WAY YOU GOTTA PLAY

Close your eyes. Imagine the Worst.

Art is Dead. Music is Dead. There is nothing to laugh about. Nothing to cry about. Nothing to enjoy. The world is broken, void of creativity. Everything that was once flamboyant now seems ordinary. The empire has no clothes.

But there are still whole other worlds inside your head. Think about them for a moment. Every dark fantasy, every bright daydream, every grim nightmare you've had. It's time to gouge them out of your imagination, make music having never heard any music, draw pictures having never seen a drawing. Write that stuff down, draw it on the back of a napkin. You have no frame of reference because your frame of reference has been thrown on the bonfire — where it belongs. There are no franchises now other than the ones locked up in the meat locker inside your mind. Walt Disney is dead. The STAR WARS are over. James Bond's license has been revoked and somebody squished SPIDER-MAN. What took so long? Because in the worlds inside YOUR head YOU cannot die. When you create something new you live forever, or at least until the next guy turns his imagination inside out and makes yours look like Wonder Bread.

This comic made my brain hurt, but Art is supposed to do that — it's supposed to stir your loins, not just tickle your fancy — it has to be the chic mala in a world of homely girls. It has to be beautiful and dangerous. Claudio Sanchez, Chondra Echert and Sheldon Vella have thrown us a bone here. They're good people, sweethearts really, but this book is not for the nervous. This book does not play it safe. This book has not been sanitized for your protection — it will scrape the dark matter out of the darkest recesses of your brain and force-feed it back to you — it's so high concept it's lowbrow — it's the Mighty Boosh leaving it for beaver on the Yellow Brick Road.

If your sense of propriety is offended by KILL AUDIO then you'd better petition for someone to keep Sanchez, Echert and Mr. Sheldon far apart. You may need whole continents and oceans between them — PLANETS, maybe. Because KILL AUDIO offers you no context, no pat explanations, no rigid laws of right or wrong, no up and down or sense of gravity. KILL AUDIO offers us a world that's part Chuck Jones Porn, part Black Flag Guitar Hero and part Jazz-flavored Pringles.

It's like a shot of bourbon up the nose out of a spraycan.

It's like broken bloody nails on a chalkboard.

It's black and white and read all over.

Drink lots of water.

Dig it.

— RICHARD STARKINGS

You can open your eyes now.

Richard Starkings is the creator of Image Comics' hit series Elephantmen and the Eisner Award-winning series Hip Flask. Although he lettered Batman: The Killing Joke with a pen, Starkings is perhaps best known for his work with the Comicraft Design and Lettering Studio, which he co-founded in 1992.

THE CAST

BONE BEAVER:
A skeleton in a beaver costume with a deep love of music history. "Beav" is the resident genre expert. He and DJ Bedroom are like brothers.

CHOOCH:
A drunk, squeaky newspaper with low self-esteem and a filthy mouth, Chooch worked at the Clocktower as a chew toy for Clockwork's dogs. He advertises his indiscretions on the changing news headlines on his chest.

CLOCKWORK:
The creator of Sight & Sound, with a Type A personality, Clockwork is also responsible for developing the Void. He believes S & S is a better place when it's perfectly controlled.

DEMISE O'DRAMA:
Demure and sweet, Demise controls the Theater and Performing Arts chapter of the Void. Her hair is partially alive, reflecting her changing moods and emotions.

CHICKEN COKE DADDY (CHI-CO):
A sex-starved, oversized chicken with delusions of grandeur and a sweet tooth for cocaine and women, but a lover deep down.

SWITCH:
Lamp's partner in crime-fighting, turned personal assistant.

ART MURDER:
Dashing, painfully hip, and the eldest of the Void, Art is the creative counterbalance for Fine Art. He is the obvious favorite of Clockwork and seems to have patrolling creativity down perfectly.

FIXLER:
The most resourceful creature in S & S, he is perplexed by Kill Audio's inability to die and constantly looking for a way to "fix" him.

LAMP:
A one time super hero turned real estate mogul, Lamp is Distress's ex-husband and a real control freak.

DJ BEDROOM:
The sleepy hip-hop pillow with a heart of gold, DJ is equal parts rationality and innocence. His intellect and passion for basketball usually get him out of sticky situations.

DISTRESS:
Former wife of the Lamp, Distress is a double-headed Siren with a bit of a sadistic bone in her body as her specialty was once luring in men with song and killing them. Her father is the ruler of the water worlds.

KILL AUDIO (KA):
He's a smartass midget with no musical creativity since Clockwork developed him to control the musical sector of the Void. Mysteriously missing for many years, he has a big job ahead of him getting music in line. Good thing he's immortal.

ANGEL OF DEATH (AOD):
Kill Audio's talking belt buckle, who not only stores musical genres, but is an all-inclusive categorical system. AOD is a snob whose only joy in life is to give KA a hard time.

WRIT END:
Writ controls Written Word within the Void. As he has no grasp of syntax, his grammar is awful, but don't let it fool you — he's very intelligent.

THE FATHERS
(ROCK, JAZZ, FOLK, CLASSICAL, ELECTRONIC):
They are the founders of all music in Sight & Sound and the only logical creators of the ever-growing population of sub-genres.

CHAPTER 1

I CAN HANDLE CHAOS...
...BUT THIS IS JUST ANNOYING.

AND KNIVES THROWING KNIVES? THAT'S YOUR BEST SHOT AT SURREALISM?

AT LEAST WHEN DALI DID IT THERE WAS A MELTING JESUS OR A SMOKING HOT CHICK.

COULDN'T EVEN MAKE THIS INTERESTING. WELL, IF NOTHING ELSE, I GUESS MY CHUNKY ASS COULD USE THE CARDIO.

EASY, FUGGERS- THAT HURTS!
SHNK! SHNK-SHNK!

NEED FIXING?
COME ON, FIX-LER, NOT AGAIN...

I MISJUDGED YOU, FIX. YOU ARE A JACKASS.
ALL THIS TIME WASTED ON THE IMPOSSIBLE. WHY DON'T YOU DO SOMETHING PRODUCTIVE?...
...YOU KNOW, PLANT SOME TREES, LEARN TO FISH, DROP A DEUCE IN YOUR HAND AND LOOK AT IT... WHATEVER MOVES YA.
OH, COME ON! NOW YOU'RE JUST BEING MEAN.
WELL, WE'VE BEEN THROUGH AT LEAST A DOZEN OF THESE LITTLE ATTEMPTS AND YOU DON'T SEEM TO GET IT--
--I CAN NOT DIE!
SERIOUSLY?
I HAD TO TRY. YOU JUST LOOKED SO VULNERABLE.
SPLUT!

VULNERABLE?
FOR A DUDE WHO'S ALWAYS TRYING TO OFF MY ASS, YOU SURE TALK LIKE YOU HAVE A SET OF GRAPE NUTS FOR TESTICLES.
HUH?
NEVERMIND. JUST PLEASE TRY TO FIND A HOBBY THAT DOESN'T INVOLVE ME.
KANG!
HEY MAN, I'M SORRY IF I'M BEING ANNOYING, BUT IT'S KIND OF WHAT I'M HERE FOR.
IT'S MY PURPOSE.
MAYBE YOU NEED TO FIND SOME DIRECTION OF YOUR OWN.
WHAT?
YOUR PURPOSE.
SINCE YOU HAVE THIS GIFT FOR DEFYING MORTALITY, SOME-ONE MUST HAVE BIGGER PLANS FOR YOU.
YOU KNOW, YOU'RE RIGHT. MAYBE YOU'RE NOT SUCH A WORTHLESS TOOL AFTER ALL, FIX.
SO--
SEE YA NEXT TRY?
I'M COUNTING DOWN THE HOURS.

A PURPOSE. THAT'S WHAT I NEED. MY REASON FOR BEING HERE--
--AND THERE'S ONLY ONE PLACE I CAN GO FOR THAT.
TO THE HEART OF THIS WRETCHED WORLD, TO THE WATCHTOWER, TO HIM...
POOM!
...CLOCKWORK: THE CREATOR OF ALL SIGHT AND SOUND.
I know a place where we can dance the whole
THE FACT THAT I HAVE NO IDEA HOW TO GET THERE, POSES A PROBLEM.
BUT THERE'S GOT TO BE SOMEONE WHO KNOWS THIS PLACE IN AND OUT.
YEAH, BABY!
BRING THAT DOODLE-DOO OVER TO THIS POPPY-COCK!

Come with me and we can shake your blues away
HEY, UH, WHO ARE YOU TALKING TO?
you'll be doin' music
OH!!
OH! YOU STARTLED ME, BABY!
MY FAULT. HEY, YOU GOT A SECOND TO BREAK AWAY FROM THAT FINE PIECE OF PAIL YOU GOT THERE?
I WAS WONDERING IF YOU COULD TELL ME THE QUICKEST ROUTE TO THE WATCHTOWER?
WHY DELAY WITH SUCH FOOLISH QUESTIONS?
THE MUSIC'S GOT ALL THE ANSWERS YOU NEED. GO ON, GRAB A CHICK 'N' STICK, BABY.
THERE'S ENOUGH TO GO ROUND. BUH-COCK!
To the beat of the rhythm of
NIGHT? CHICKS? MAN, IT'S MORNING AND THERE'S NO ONE HERE EXCEPT YOU, ME AND SOME TRASH. I HATE TO BREAK IT TO YA BUDDY, BUT THIS ISN'T A CLUB--
--IT'S SOMEONE ELSE'S CRAP!
BUDDY? NAME'S NOT BUDDY, YOU DISRESPECTFUL DWARF BASTARD.
YOU ARE IN THE PRESENCE OF THE GODFATHER OF BLOW, MOTHER-CLUCKER!
CONQUEROR OF THE MIGHTY MOUNT COKE-AMENJARO!
SO YA BETTA' SEIZE THAT TONGUE AND RECOGNIZE, BEE-ITCH!
MY NAME'S CHICKEN COKE DADDY! BUH-COCK!

DUDE, WILL YOU GET THAT SLUG OUT OF MY FACE?
BRACE YOURSELF, FOOL!
JUST STOP IT ALREADY, YOU COKED OUT COCK!
Z.

LISTEN, I'M SORRY BUT YOUR ERRATIC BEHAVIOR WAS DRIVING ME UP A WALL.

I JUST NEED SOME HELP AND BY THE LOOKS OF IT YOU COULD PROBABLY USE SOME TOO.

HELP? WHAT YOU TALKING 'BOUT? REHAB? DAMN, YOU CRAZY!

WHATEVER. I'M GOING TO THE WATCHTOWER TO HAVE A WORD WITH CLOCKWORK TO FIGURE OUT MY PURPOSE. IF ANYTHING I COULD USE THE COMPANY.

YOU INTERESTED?

?

YOU AIN'T GOING TO SUCKA ME INTO NO INTERVENTION, ARE YA?

MOMMA CHICKEN YOU HIDIN' IN THIS DUMPSTER!?

YOU'RE THE MASTER OF YOUR OWN, CHI-CO.

CHI-CO? HEY, I LIKE THAT. WHAT'S YOUR NAME, LITTLE MAN?

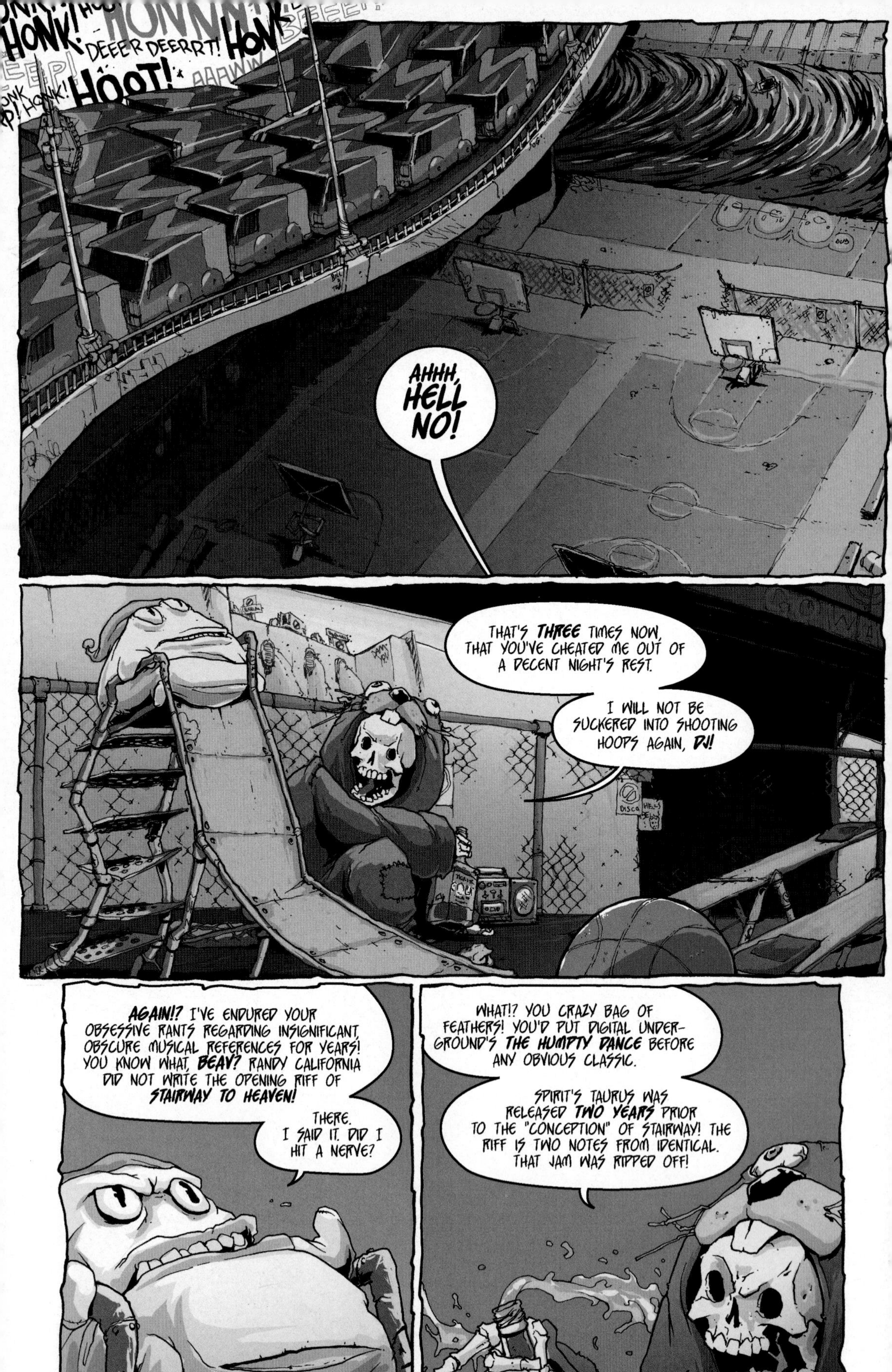
HONK! HOONK! DEEER DEERRT! HONK! HOOT! HONK!
AHHH, HELL NO!
THAT'S THREE TIMES NOW, THAT YOU'VE CHEATED ME OUT OF A DECENT NIGHT'S REST.
I WILL NOT BE SUCKERED INTO SHOOTING HOOPS AGAIN, DJ!
AGAIN!? I'VE ENDURED YOUR OBSESSIVE RANTS REGARDING INSIGNIFICANT, OBSCURE MUSICAL REFERENCES FOR YEARS! YOU KNOW WHAT, BEAV? RANDY CALIFORNIA DID NOT WRITE THE OPENING RIFF OF STAIRWAY TO HEAVEN!
THERE. I SAID IT. DID I HIT A NERVE?
WHAT!? YOU CRAZY BAG OF FEATHERS! YOU'D PUT DIGITAL UNDER-GROUND'S THE HUMPTY DANCE BEFORE ANY OBVIOUS CLASSIC.
SPIRIT'S TAURUS WAS RELEASED TWO YEARS PRIOR TO THE "CONCEPTION" OF STAIRWAY! THE RIFF IS TWO NOTES FROM IDENTICAL. THAT JAM WAS RIPPED OFF!
MONSTER

BEST TWO OUT OF THREE?

A SHOT IN TH DARK

GOLF

GET A LAWYER SON

THE BEAV'S FAVORITE GAME OF ALL TIME. ***DEEP CUTS* INVOLVES ROCKING OUT, WHILE HEAVILY INTOXICATED, TO WHATEVER YOUR OPPONENT'S SONG CHOICES MAY BE-- WHETHER YOU LIKE THEM OR NOT.

WELL THERE AIN'T A WHOLE LOTTA OPTIONS.
HARDLY THE DYNAMIC DUO, NOT THAT WE'RE SETTING THE BAR TOO HIGH...
TO FIND THE WAY YOU GOTTA PLAY, BABY!
ALRIGHT THEN. LOSE THE GLASSES. THEY'RE NOT GOING TO TAKE US SERIOUSLY WITH YOU LOOKIN' LIKE ERIC ESTRADA.
COME ON.
MAN, I WAS FEELIN' MORE STALLONE IN COBRA.
HUH?
ANY LUCK?
YOU GOT TO BE KIDDIN' ME.

CHAK
RACKLE!
KILLING YOU
I AM.
KIDDING YOU
I AM NOT.
RKL
RK
SURKL
IT'S DAYS LIKE THESE...
DA
BOOSH

...THAT IMMORTALITY'S A REAL BITCH...

10 DAYS PASS...
HOOOLD MY BREATH--
--AS I WISH FOR DEEEAAA-TH...
SP-DOOSH!
OH QUIT YOUR SNIFFLING!
!?
SNAG

BAD ENOUGH I HAVE TO COME SAVE YOUR LITTLE ASS...
SPLOOSH!
...BUT I REFUSE TO HEAR YOU BUTCHER A JAM SO DEAR TO MY HEART.
HOW IN THE--
SHRIIIIP!!
THANKS. HOW IN THE HELL DID YOU GET THESE TWO INVOLVED?
WELL, FIRRRRRRST...

...I CRUSHED THE FATTEST LINE WEST OF THIS DIRTY WORLD. GLORIOUS SHE WAS, A SOFT RIVER OF ANGEL'S DRUFF!
SNRRKT
A BUMP SO FINE SHE RIVALED THE GREAT WALL AND COULD POTENTIALLY BLOW A CHICKEN'S HARD-ON TO SMITHEREENS.
I GET THE POINT, CHICO.
I DON'T THINK YOU DO, KA.
I MEAN HOW THE HELL WAS I GONNA COMPETE WITH THESE TWO ALONE? I WAS OUT NUMBERED AND WAAAAY OUT SKILLED. I NEEDED ASSISTANCE, BABY.
AND OLD GLORIA, WELL, SHE WAS THERE TO PROVIDE.
SO, I DESTROYED ANOTHER ONE! BAM!
THEN LADIES & GENTLEMEN--

--SHOWTIME!

AIIIGHT, YOU BITCH ASS NECTARINES!

WHICH COURT YA'LL PLAYIN'?

KURT WAS HERE '96

UNFORTUNATELY, MY 'SUBCONSCICAL' MIND GOT THE BEST AND THAT BEAVER SET SOMETHING LOOSE.

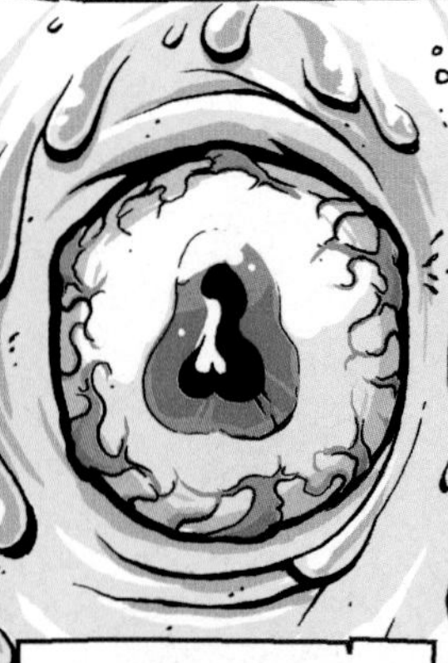

SUDDENLY I HAD THIS VENOMOUS, UNSTOPPABLE URGE TO **CLUCK.**

BORN TO BE ALIVE
HEY THERE, PICKEN-SLIM.
OH!?
ITS GOOD TO BE ALIVE
LOOKS LIKE YOU COULD USE A RIDE.

NOTHING SAYS STUFFING LIKE STOVETOP...
...MY SWEET HONEY GLAZED!
HUMP! HUMP! HUMP!
THAT CHICKEN IS GOING TO LOSE HIS TENDER IF WE DON'T DO SOMETHING QUICK.
GIMME THAT BALL.
WHIP!
FWUMP!
TENG
TENG

I GUESS YOU COULD SAY THE REST IS HISTORY.
CHALK IT UP TO ANOTHER ONE OF DJ'S CHARITY CASE DRAMAS.
ANOTHER? YOU MEAN TO TELL ME THIS IS A COMMON PROBLEM FOR YOU?
HELL YEAH! POLYESTER FILL OVER HERE HAS A MOTHER THERESA COMPLEX.

WELL, HOP ON BOARD THE DISASTER TRAIN, MY FRIENDS.
WE'RE HEADED TO FIND **CLOCKWORK** AND I'M SURE THERE'LL BE MORE THAN ENOUGH FIASCOS TO KEEP YOU TWO BUSY ON THE WAY.
BESIDES, THAT LITTLE TRICK YOU DID BACK THERE COULD BE A GREAT SOURCE OF ENTERTAINMENT.
NO THANKS. I WASN'T BORN A RAMBLIN' MAN IF YOU KNOW WHAT I MEAN. LIKE TO STAY CLOSE TO THE BEAVER DAM.

LET'S GO, DJ.

IT'S COOL. I'M SURE WE CAN FIND **SOMEONE ELSE** TO HANDLE THE MUSICAL ACCOMPANIMENT ON THE ROAD...
YESSS!

PLAY

Leaving home ain't easy

THIS JAM IS KINDA DEPRESSING.

WELL DO YOU HAVE A BETTER SUGGESTION?

I Never Thought it would be easy

HOW ABOUT MORRICONE? **MAN WITH NO NAME** TYPE O' SHREDS.

EH, HOW ABOUT THIS-

A FEW HOURS LATER...

A LITTLE **WHITNEY** NEVER HURT ANYONE.

OOH I WANNA DANCE

HOW APPROPRIATE.

WITH SOME BOD

DAMN BABY!

I DIDN'T REALIZE WE WALKED **THIS** FAR.

ENTER THE GATES TO HELL IS WHERE WITH US DWE

WHAT **IS** THIS?

THE REASON I STAY HOME--
--AREN'T THOSE OBITUARY LYRICS?
CAN YOU HOLD OFF ON THE TRIVIA PLEASE?
PLEASING CAN ONLY BRING PLEASURE--
--THERE AIN'T NONE OF THAT ON THIS ENDEAVOR, PLAYAS.
WE'RE HERE. THE TORRENT GATES.
GOOD NEWS IS WE'RE ON THE RIGHT PATH TO THE TOWER. UNFORTUNATELY, BITCHES, THIS AIN'T NO YELLOW BRICK ROAD.
HOW DO YOU KNOW THAT?
USED TO RUN WITH BILLY "TOUCAN" FANDANGO. REAL KNOCKOUT WITH THE LADIES. TOLD ME HE'D BRING 'EM UP HERE FOR A LITTLE WIGGLY WOO IN THE POO POO 'NAH MEAN, FEATHERS?
DOINK DOINK
I DON'T THINK I WANT TO GO IN.
I DON'T THINK THEM GIRLS DID EITHER.
WELL IF YOU GUYS WANT TO SIT OUT HERE ALL NIGHT RAPPIN' ABOUT NOTHING, HAVE FUN, BUT I DIDN'T COME HERE FOR THE TALE OF A HOMELESS TOUCAN'S LIBIDO.
BURRRR-ITO!!
JUST TRYING TO BREAK THE ICE.

SLOW DOWN, BABY!
YOU GUYS WERE ALL WORKED UP ABOUT COMING THROUGH HERE AND FOR WHAT?
FUGGIN' CITY FOLK CAN'T HANDLE THE FRESH AIR.
IT STILL GIVES ME THE HEEBIE JEEBIES.
FROM CHI-CO'S STORY, SOUNDS LIKE IT'LL GIVE YOU A LOT MORE TH THAT, DJ. YOU BETTER WATCH YOUR POLYESTER ASS.
CLOSER NO HES TATION
GIVE me ALL The YOU HA

POP!
POP!
WAKED MY THOUGHTS
RE
REEPING
KARR
TOO LATE
THE SHOW HAS BEGUN
SNAP!
OOP!
MILK

DAMMIT!
YOUR JEALOUSY HAS DESTROYED OUR DECOY FOR THE LAST TIME!
BUT DARLING...
YIPE!
YIPE!
YIP
...I WAS JUST GOING TO CHECK ON THE PROGRESS-- FOR YOUR SAFETY.
YOU'RE NOTHING BUT AN INSECURE, PATHOLOGICAL LIAR. I SHOULD HAVE KNOWN THIS TRIAL SEPARATION WOULDN'T WORK.
I WANT OUT!
WELL THEN THAT MAKES TWO OF US!

YOU CAN KEEP THIS OVERGROWN EXCUSE FOR AN EVIL FOREST. ANYTHING BEHIND THE TORRENT GATES IS ALL YOURS, SWEETHEART. I'M TAKING THE CITY APARTMENT-
-AND THE WAKEES.
"WAKEES"
CHILL BABY, THAT'S NO WAY TO HANDLE A FINE LADY ...OR TWO.
IF YOU FIND A LADY AROUND HERE, GIVE ME A CALL.
SLAM!
PRICK!
DOK
SO IT WOULD APPEAR CHIVALRY ISN'T DEAD. AND FOR THAT, MAYBE YOU HANDSOME GENTLEMEN AREN'T EITHER.
TYPICALLY, I WOULD INVITE YOU IN THEN DIVERT YOUR PLANS BY CUTTING YOUR HEARTS FROM YOUR CHEST.
BUT IT SEEMS MY NEW BACHELORETTE STATUS HAS ME FEELING CHARITABLE.
WE'RE HEADED TO-

HUSH LOVE, I KNOW WHERE YOU'RE GOING.
EVERYONE WHO GETS THIS FAR IS GOING TO THE SAME PLACE.
I'M WILLING TO GIVE YOU THE OPTION TO GET THERE. ALL IT'LL TAKE IS A KISS. I HAVE SUCH A WEAK SPOT FOR SMALL, DARK AND OBNOXIOUS.
BUT IT'S UP TO YOU TO DECIDE WHICH SIDE GETS IT. YOU SEE, IT'S NOT JUST MY SONG THAT'S DEADLY.
ONE PAIR OF LIPS ARE MADE OF THE PUREST POISON. THE OTHER HOLD YOUR TICKET OF SAFE PASSAGE TO CLOCKWORK.
THEY SAY LOVE IS A RISK? PROVE IT.
WELL THAT WAS DELICIOUS WASN'T IT? AND LITTLE MAN-
KILL AUDIO.
-YES, KILL AUDIO, I'M AWARE YOU CAN'T DIE.
TELL THAT OLD WIZARD DISTRESS SENDS HER REGARDS.

THE TOWER
WHA' THE FUG ARE YOU TWO LOOKIN' AT?
YOU THINK I'M A JOKE?
SNIFF WELL I AM.
SQUEEK
BUFFALO WING ENEMA
GO AHEAD AND LAUGH AT THE CHOOCH.
HURF HURFFF RURF
MAYBE THEY'RE JUST LOOKIN' TO PARTY?
ARE YOU FUGGIN' NUTS!? THAT BLOW WILL SEND THOSE THINGS INTO TWICE THE RAGING FIT THEY'RE ALREADY IN.
THINK, COKE, THINK.
I ALWAYS DO, BABY! BUH-COCK!
SNRRRKT!
BROWH
LOOK AT THE PAIR ON THAT THING!
SIZE AINT NOTHING. STEP ASIDE I'LL SHOW YA REAL BALLS. WHO'S GOT A LIGHTER?
SQUEE
CHAK CHAK

YO, FORGIVE ME IF I'M WRONG BUT ISN'T HE A DOG'S CHEW TOY?
YEAH.
AND HE'S PRETTY MUCH LEAKING WHISKEY...
UH HUH.
THEN WHAT ARE WE WAITING FOR? IF HE INTENDS TO LIGHT HIS TESTES ON FIRE, THAT BOOZE IS GOING TO BURN OFF INSTANTLY.
OH, HELL NO!
EMOTIONALLY DISTURBED HOOKER
PUNT
RULF!
AAAA...
ROW! ROW! BOLF! OLF!
ULP GULP ULP...
ULP ULP
GUUURP
JUURRP
ZZZ
ROCK 'N' ROLL CHOOCHIE-CHOO!
ZZZZZZ
I THINK I MAY HAVE SQUIRTED MORE THAN ALCOHOL.
CH-CHAK!

clock work
clock work
only way is up
FRUFF
SWRRKT!
UGH!
PANT!
WRRRKT! AAAH
BEAV, C'MON!
EAT IT, DJ.
CLOCKWORK
HUFF HUFF HUFF...
HUFF UFF...
OFFICE OF
CLOCKWORK
KEEPER OF
SIGHT & SOUND
DO NOT DISTURB

CAN'T BELIEVE WE MADE IT HERE.
I THINK I SHOULD DO THIS ALONE-
BLAM

IN MY DEFENSE, I THOUGHT THE PLAYING FIELD MIGHT BE LEVEL HERE.
THE PRESENCE OF THE ALMIGHTY COULD MAKE YOU MORTAL OR SOMETHING.
SPLOOB!

I'LL WAIT OUT HERE JUST IN CASE.
POP!

WELL I'LL BE DAMNED IF WE JUST TRAIPSED 1000 MILES TO WAIT IT OUT WITH CAPTAIN DILDO HERE. I FOR ONE, AM COMING IN.

EVEN THOUGH IT WAS MORE LIKE 9 MILES, I'D LIKE TO JOIN YOU TOO KA.

GOTTA AGREE WITH THE DJ, LITTLE MAN.

THIS COCK WOULD LOSE SOME SERIOUS SLEEP IF YOU GO GETTIN' CREEPED ON BY SOME WHITE WIZARD.

BESIDES, YOU COULD FIND OUT YOU'RE SOME KINDA ROYALTY OR THE LAST REMAINING OF AN ALIEN MIDGET RACE.

POINT BEING, WE GOTTA DO THIS **TOGETHER**, LITTLE HOMIE.

BE MY GUEST.

TOK TIK TOK CHOK TIK TIK
KLOK CHUK TOK TIK
TOK TOK TIK TOK
KILL AUDIO! MY LANDS BOY, WHERE HAVE YOU BEEN?!
'SCUSE ME?

TIK
MUSIC HAS BECOME AN ABSOLUTE CATASTROPHE SINCE YOU'VE BEEN GONE. THEY'RE ON THE CUSP OF TAKING OVER EVERYTHING! I SIMPLY CANNOT CONTROL THEM ALONE MUCH LONGER!
WAIT A MINUTE, WAIT A MINUTE.
ALL HELL'S BROKEN LOOSE, AND YOU'VE BEEN LOOKIN'...

...FOR THIS GUY?

WOT.

DOING!

TOK
WELL OF COURSE! ORDER SHALL BE RESTORED NOW THAT YOU'VE RETURNED TO US.

LISTEN. YOU OBVIOUSLY HAVE A WHOLE LOTTA PROBLEMS OF YOUR OWN AND SEEING AS HOW I CAME HERE FOR GUIDANCE, NOT MORE CONFUSION IN MY OWN CLUSTERFUG OF A LIFE, I THINK MAYBE WE SHOULD BE GOING.

BUT KILL AUDIO, THIS IS YOUR PURPOSE. I BEG YOU TO HEAR ME OUT.
THE DELICATE BALANCE OF LIFE AND CREATIVITY IN THE LAND OF SIGHT AND SOUND DEPENDS ON IT.
TOK
TIK
CHFFF...
SNKT!
WE'RE ALL EARS, GEARS.
TOK
TIK
TIK
T-TOK
TOK
THE ISSUES WITH MUSIC HAVE SNOWBALLED OVER THE DECADES INTO THIS MESS, BUT IT CAN ALL BE TRACED BACK TO ONE SINGLE EVENT-
-THE DAY YOU WERE TAKEN FROM THE VOID.
SO YOU'RE SAYING ALL THESE PROBLEMS YOU'RE HAVING WITH MUSIC OR WHATEVER, ARE MY FAULT?
NO, YOU SILLY CHAP.
TSSSSS

YOU ARE
THE ONLY
SOLUTION.

TIME TO FACE
THE MUSIC

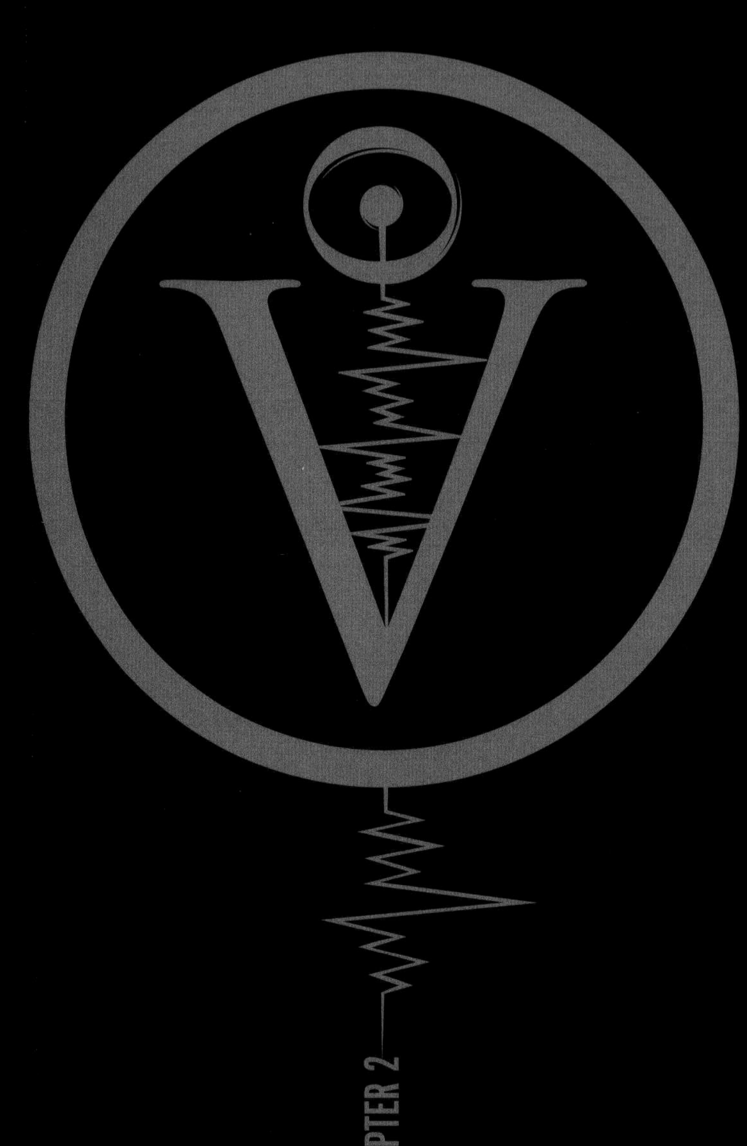

CHAPTER 2

SPUDGE
SSNORRRT
SMUDGE
SMUDGE
GLAK
SP-TOO!
THIP!
THUP!
SPUTZ!

I'M SURPRISED YOU MADE IT.

THOUGHT YOU'D BE A NO SHOW.
SKRT
SKRT
SKRT

I CAN STAND AS MUCH OF THAT SNIVELLIN' BABY AS I CAN OF YOU!
BUT IF SOMEONE'S MUCKIN' ABOUT WITH MY FAMILY, I'M ALL ABOUT GETTING ANGRY AND EVEN.
SO OUT WITH IT. WHERE'S THE KID?
FLINK!
SSSSP!
FOOOO
I HAVE A STORY TO TELLLLL--
--THE NIGHT WAS BLACK LIKE A SUN SCORCHED HEART... THE BROTHERRRR OF TEARS SLEPT SOUNDLY --
OI!!
SAVE THE CRYPTIC WEIRDO SING-SONG RUBBISH AND GET ON WITH IT, WILL YA?

IT WAS A TYPICAL DAY FOR HIM. GOT INTO A FIGHT WITH POP, CAME HOME IN TEARS AND LOCKED HIMSELF IN HIS ROOM TO PLAY THAT TERRIBLE ACOUSTIC ALL NIGHT.
I'M NOT DEAD
AT 11, THE MUSIC STOPPED. I ASSUMED HE WAS TAKING PICTURES OF HIMSELF AS USUAL. HE ALWAYS SAID EYE-LINER RUNNING DOWN HIS FACE WAS A SIGN OF REAL PAIN AND HE HAD TO CAPTURE IT IMMEDIATELY.
I WENT TO WAKE HIM IN THE MORNING...
FWUP!
BUT HE WAS JUST GONE.
KLOKKA
LITTLE TOSSER'S RUN OFF FOR ATTENTION, PROBABLY.
PFFT
PFFT!
PFFT
I CONSIDERED THAT. BUT HE ALWAYS LEAVES SOME MELO-DRAMATIC NOTE.
BOLLOCKS
PFFT!
SO I SEARCHED HIS ROOM FOR ANY CLUES OF THE USUAL SUSPECTS. YOU KNOW, WIZARDRY, WARLOCKS, VENGEFUL CENTAURS--

THE DEMON SPAWNED A DEMON CHILD--
--BLOODY HELL!!
NONE OF THOSE TOOK 'IM 'COZ NONE OF THOSE DON'T FOOGIN' EXIST! YOU'RE WASTING TIME I COULD BE DEVOTING TO MAYHEM.
DOINK!
ANARCHY DOESN'T HAPPEN OVERNIGHT.
THE VOID-HE'S BACK.
THEN I FOUND THIS.
SO...
SO WHAT DO YOU KNOW ABOUT THIS WANKER?

KER-RAAASH
DONK
YOU'RE ABOUT TO BE TOKED LIKE CALIFORNIA CORNFLAKES,
SUCKAS!

BROTHER! WE MUST DEFEND TO THE DEATH!
DOUBLE WIELD!
NO FOOGIN' WAY I'M HANGIN' AROUND FOR THIS NONSENSE.
LIGHTNING BOLT!! +4 DMG!
ZANG!
SHUNK!
HAHA! STITCH IT, SHORT FLIP!
OOF!
WHUMP
THIS GUN IS STUPID. WHOSE IDEA WAS THIS AGAIN?
THOOM
CHAK!
K-SPOOGE!
OH!
IT WORKS DOESN'T IT?
I GET IT BABY, I'M A CHICKEN, BUT I AIN'T NO EGG-LAYIN' LADY.
GAKK!
OH-GOD!
ACTUALLY CHI-CO...

CHICKENS ARE BY DEFAULT, UM, LADIES. MALES ARE TECHNICALLY ROOS-
-TERS.
SPOOGE!
SHLUK
WOULD YOU TWO STOP DICK-ING AROUND? HE'S GETTING AWAY!
BLURG!
UNIHORN
CHINK
UNIHORN
YOU STILL WANT TO PLAY WITH SWORDS, LANCELOT?
TRIP!
SPLAT!
CUZ I GOT ONE FOR YA.
DONK!

NO! NO!! NO!
BY THE POWER OF GREYSKULL I DEMAND YOU LEAVE ME!
CLOK!

SORRY, KID. BEEN OFF THE JOB TOO LONG TO SLACK OFF SO SOON.
ENGAGE

SNKT!

SERIOUSLY, ARE WE REALLY DOING THIS AGAIN?

CAN'T-YOU-DISPLAY ME-SOMEPLACE-ELSE? I-DON'T-APPRECIATE BEING-SO-CLOSE-TO YOUR---PENIS.

YOU PUT YOURSELF THERE, REMEMBER?

I CAN'T BELIEVE WE'RE STILL HAVING THIS DISCUSSION.
VERY-WELL ---BITCH.

ZWII

NO!
NO!

R.RWD II
WHAT'S THE VOID?
ONLY THE MOST IMPORTANT PART OF THIS WORLD.
PLEASE ALLOW ME TO EXPLAIN. 20 MINUTES IS ALL WE NEED.
BEING ON TIME IS VERY IMPORTANT TO ME AS YOU CAN TELL.
KLOK TICK TOK TINK CHINK TINK TIC TICK TIK TOK CHOK
TOK TICK
THE ACT OF CREATION, IN ALL OF ITS FORMS, IS A VERY POTENT AND BEAUTIFUL FORCE. BUT IT CAN EASILY SPIRAL OUT OF SIMPLE INGENUITY--
--AND INTO A DARK PLACE.
EVEN I WAS VULNERABLE TO THE THREAT OF THE RAMPANT IMAGINATION WHEN FASHIONING SIGHT AND SOUND, EONS AGO.
xxx

SO I DESIGNED A BEING TO BALANCE ALL THE CREATIVITY THIS WORLD WOULD COME TO KNOW.
HE WAS THE ABSENCE OF EVERYTHING INVENTIVE. A SWEET CHAP, BUT BORING LIKE YOU WOULDN'T BELIEVE--
ZAM!
--ART MURDER.
I SOON REALIZED I HAD UNDERESTIMATED THE MAGNITUDE OF CREATIVITY FLOURISHING ON S&S. ART COULDN'T MAINTAIN EQUILIBRIUM ON HIS OWN, WHAT WITH ALL THE NEW FORMS OF INVENTION--
-WRITTEN WORD, THEATER, MUSIC-
-THESE WERE SUBJECTS I'D NEVER ANTICIPATED.
THUS, THE VOID WAS BORN. EACH WITH A SPECIAL DEFICIENCY TO STABILIZE IN EACH AREA.
THE VO
LOOK KA, THERE YOU ARE WITH YOUR BROTHERS AND SISTER. THAT'S ART, DEMISE AND WRIT. DO YOU REMEMBER THEM?
THE VOID
NOT IN THE SLIGHTEST.
IF WE WERE SUCH A WONDER TEAM, HOW COME THINGS ARE SO MESSED UP?
HAH!
HE LOOKS LIKE GIZMO!

THE SYSTEM WOULD HAVE WORKED BEAUTIFULLY WITH TIME HAD YOU NOT DISAPPEARED. WE EXPLORED EVERY CLUE AS TO WHERE YOU'D BEEN TAKEN.
SIGHT AND SOUND WAS NEARLY TORN UPSIDE DOWN IN THE SEARCH. BUT WITH EACH NEW LEAD CAME DISAPPOINTMENT AND WHILE WE GRIEVED, MUSIC TOOK ADVANTAGE, YOU SEE.
TICK TICK TOK CHOK TOK TIK TOK CHOK TOK TICK
KSHH!
DON'T YOU THINK IT'S WEIRD I HAVE NO MEMORY OF WHAT HAPPENED?
PAT! PAT!
NONE OF THAT MATTERS NOW, KILL AUDIO. YOU'VE COME BACK TO US.
IS THIS A PART OF MY COSTUME? JUST SO YOU KNOW, I'M APPLE SHAPED. I'LL LOOK LIKE A SAUSAGE IN A PAIR OF TIGHTS.
QUIT-IT-DAMMIT I-SUFFER-FROM MOTION-SICKNESS.
RITTLE RATTLE
ZRRT!
THAT'S MORE A TOOL THAN A COSTUME.
OOF!
SNAP
EACH OF THE VOID HAS ONE. BE FORE-WARNED, YOURS HAS A POOR SENSE OF HUMOR.
THE BELT COLLECTS GENRES ON THE TAPE HERE, WHICH CONVERTS TO A DIRECTORY FOR CLASSIFYING GENRES.
YOU'LL RETURN IT TO ME WHEN YOU'RE FINISHED AND I WILL GRANT CREATIVITY BACK TO THOSE I SEE AS **DESERVING.**

F.FWD »

FRUFF.

BORK!

ME.

WHAT-BUSINESS-HAVE YOU-WITH-ME? WHY-HAVE YOU-CALLED-UPON-THE **ANGEL-OF DEATH!?**

CLICK!

WHERE THE FUG DID YOU COME UP WITH THAT? YOU DON'T KILL ANY-THING.

I-AM-THE-HARVESTER OF-SOULS! I-AM-THE LIGHT-THAT-COMES-AFTER-THE DARK!
NOOO, WHAT YOU ARE IS AN OVERSIZED CATALOGUING UNIT, SO DO YOUR JOB OR WE'LL INVEST IN SOME INDEX CARDS.
YEAH, AOD--
NOW, DRAW UP THEM JAILBIRDS!
ZEEEEEEEE
WHY'D YOU HAVE TO HUMOR HIM WITH THAT AOD GARBAGE? YOU KNOW THAT JUST EGGS HIM ON.
WAS THAT AN ATTEMPT AT A JOKE?

HARD TO BELIEVE WE NEVER NOTICED THIS MUSIC MESS BEFORE. I LIKE TO THINK I'M PRETTY PERCEPTIVE.

LOOK AT THAT SMOG. IT'S KIND OF SOOTHING IN A WEIRD WAY, HUH BONE?

WHAT? NO CRACKS AT MY MANHOOD TONIGHT?

TOO MUCH ELSE ON MY MIND.

IT'S A LITTLE TOUGH COMBATTING THE ONE THING YOU LOVE.

DON'T THINK I'VE EVER BEEN FACED WITH A CONFLICT LIKE THIS BEFORE.

IT'S NOT LIKE MUSIC IS GOING WAY. WE'RE JUST TRYING TO KEEP IT IN LINE.

YOU THINK ZAPPA THOUGHT ABOUT KEEPING HIMSELF IN LINE?

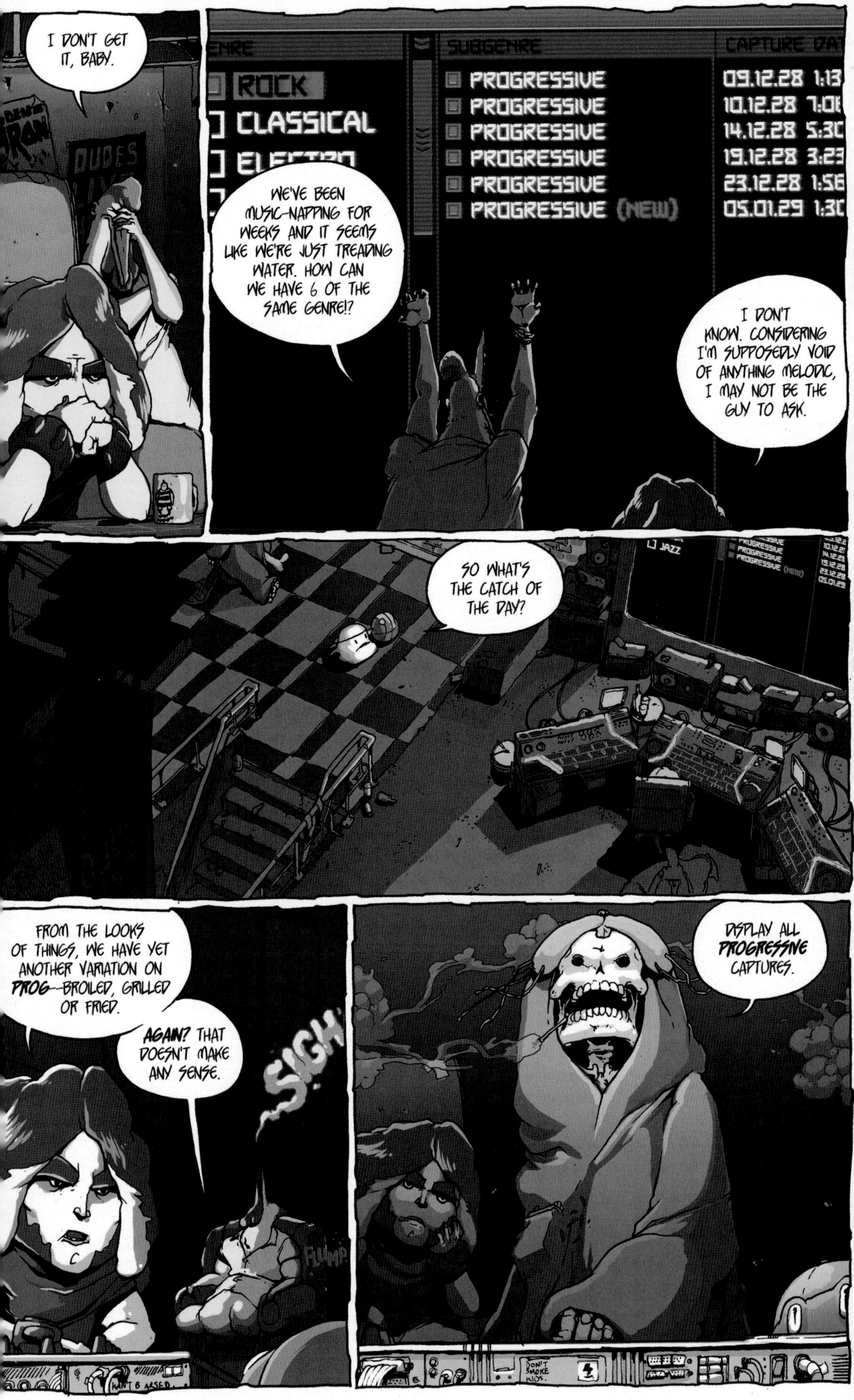

I DON'T GET IT, BABY.

SUBGENRE

ROCK
CLASSICAL

PROGRESSIVE
PROGRESSIVE
PROGRESSIVE
PROGRESSIVE
PROGRESSIVE
PROGRESSIVE (NEW)

09.12.28 1:13
10.12.28 7:0
14.12.28 5:30
19.12.28 3:23
23.12.28 1:56
05.01.29 1:30

WE'VE BEEN MUSIC-NAPPING FOR WEEKS AND IT SEEMS LIKE WE'RE JUST TREADING WATER. HOW CAN WE HAVE 6 OF THE SAME GENRE!?

I DON'T KNOW. CONSIDERING I'M SUPPOSEDLY VOID OF ANYTHING MELODIC, I MAY NOT BE THE GUY TO ASK.

SO WHAT'S THE CATCH OF THE DAY?

FROM THE LOOKS OF THINGS, WE HAVE YET ANOTHER VARIATION ON **PROG**--BROILED, GRILLED OR FRIED.

AGAIN? THAT DOESN'T MAKE ANY SENSE.

SIGH

FLUMP

KAN'T B ARSED.

DISPLAY ALL **PROGRESSIVE** CAPTURES.

DON'T SMOKE KIDS.

CAPTURES: ROCK/PROGRESSIVE
PROGRESSIVE
01
PROGRESSIVE
02
PROGRESSIVE
03
PROGRESSIVE
04
PROGRESSIVE
05
PROGRESSIVE
06
PROGRESSIVE
BLING
WELL IT MAKES SOME SENSE TO ME.
SHA-WING!
THE JOUSTING KING HERE IS CLEARLY **NEO PROG.**
AND THE GENRE WE SNAGGED TWO DAYS AGO WHILE HE DRONED ON ABOUT TIME SIGNATURES?
TAP TAP TAP
PROGRESSIVE METAL.
WHAT WOULD WE DO WITHOUT YOU?
BUT THESE OTHER FOUR ARE THROWING ME OFF. IT'S LIKE SOMEONE CHURNED THEM OUT OF A MACHINE.
BLIP!
4
"RAVER PLAYA"

SHRINKAGE!
I'VE NEVER HEARD OF PROGRESSIVE ELECTRO HOP. SURE I'D LISTEN TO IT-
BUT THE AVERAGE PERSON WOULDN'T.
IT SEEMS ILLOGICAL. WHY HAVEN'T WE CAPTURED A SINGLE FATHER YET?
FATHER?
YOU KNOW, THE BIG GUYS. LIKE CLASSICAL AND ROCK. IF A GENRE HAS ENOUGH KNOCK OFFS AND SUB-GENRES, THEY'RE CONSIDERED A FATHER.
AM I THE ONLY ONE THAT READ THE MANUAL?
I'M SURE THOSE SUBS ARE KEEPING THEIR DADDIES CLOSE TO HOME.
PROGRESSIVE
01
02
03
04
05
06
TIME TO CONSULT THE DETECTIVE.
LET'S HOPE HE'S DONE HIS HOMEWORK.

WHAT THE--
YOU'VE BEEN DRINKING THIS ENTIRE TIME!?
!!
URR- URRR-
WELL UHHH-
WELL YOU HAVEN'T GIVEN ME A WHOLE LOT TO WORK WITH SINCE YOU DRAGGED ME OUT OF THE POOCH-PIT!
I KNEW I HEARD SOMEONE MOVING AROUND HERE LAST NIGHT.
BEAV, WHERE DO YOU KEEP THE MAKER'S MARK?

ARE YOU KIDDING ME? WE GAVE YOU ALL THE NECESSARY INFORMATION, INCLUDING THAT LEAD WE HAD ON JAZZ!
DID YOU DO ANYTHING?
MOO BREW
YEAH I'LL HAVE YOU KNOW I DID A LOT OF THINGS. NOT JUST ANYTHING. AND THAT'S SOMETHING...
NEWS
HOW DARE
BEACAUSE IT'S EVERYTHING.
NEWS
OOOOOH.
OOOOO-OOOOH...
DAMN, THIS BOY NEEDS A BABYSITTER.
SKFF
The Bitches Brew
33 D.I.J.C
2ND ST
LET ME SEE THAT.
CHOOCH, DID YOU GO ANYWHERE BEFORE YOU GOT DRUNK?
SURE DID.
NEWS
AT LEAST YOU'VE GOT GOOD INTENTIONS...

The Bitches Brew
OPEN
The Bitches Brew
OPEN
CLOSED
GO HOME DAMMIT
NO COVER NO LOVER
DRUNK AS HELL
BKOM
MAN, THAT WAS 18 KARAT.
YEAH, BUT TOO MANY HIGH D'S TONIGHT.
DAP!
NO DOUBT. HAND ME SOME SKIN TIL' TOMORROW, BROTHER.
BURRP

DON'T JIVE ME, MAN!
BA
FLINK
I UNDER-STAND YOU'RE BEING CAUGHT UNAWARE. WE DIDN'T THINK HE WOULD FIND OUT HIS FUNCTION IN SIGHT AND SOUND, LET ALONE ACTUALLY COME BACK TO WORK--
--BUT I NEVER PROMISED THERE WOULD BE NO CASUALTIES.
I'M TRYING NOT TO BLOW MY TOP, BUT YOU PUT ME IN THE MIX WITHOUT THINKING ALL THE DETAILS THROUGH.
I WANTED TO BE THE MAIN MAN 'ROUND HERE, NOT A WALKIN' TARGET.
BAD ENOUGH HALF THE FATHERS' KIDS BEEN AFTER ME SINCE WE STARTED, NOW I HAVE THAT TURKEY BREATHIN' DOWN MY NECK.
PUFF
PUFF
IN THE MEANTIME, I THINK I'VE FOUND A WAY TO HELP SPEED UP PRODUCTION.
I HAVE ALREADY TAKEN PREVENTATIVE MEASURES.
PLAP!
THIS JACK LOOKS BAD!

SO WHAT'S OUR PLAN?
304
03:12am
TO BE CONTINUED...

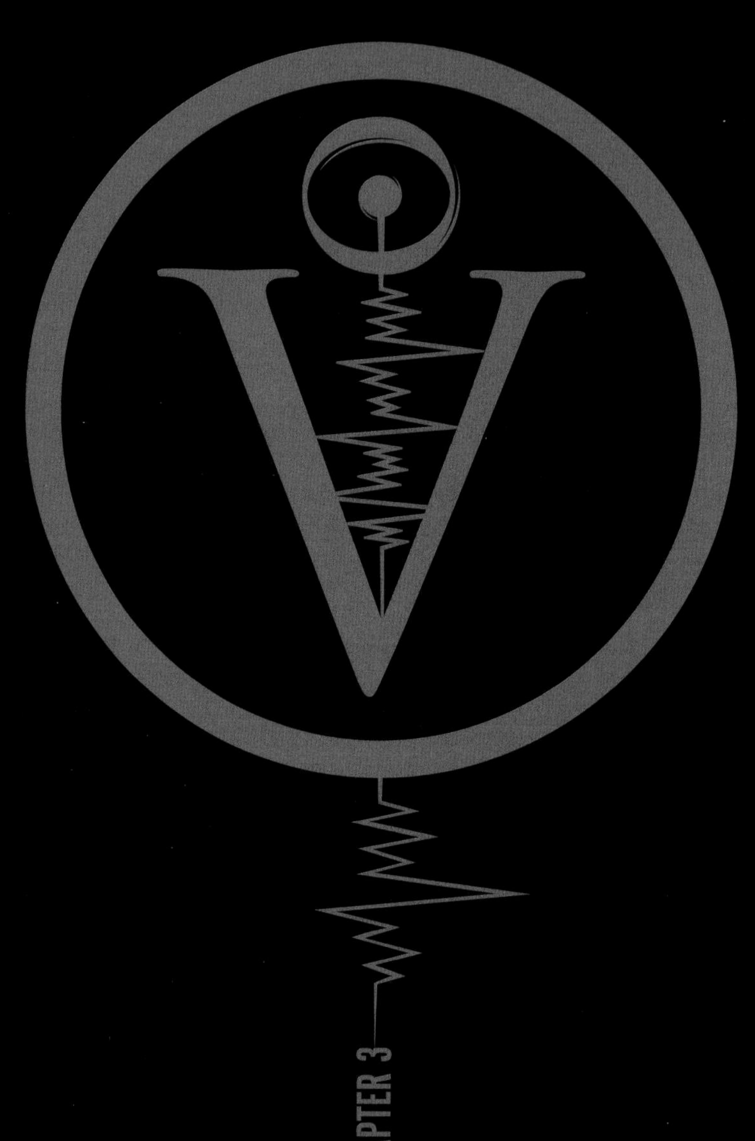

CHAPTER 3

BLOP
GLOP
SOOP
BLOOP
SWEEE
SNIPE
SLOOP
SPEEEE
FFSSSSS
SWEEE
SWEEE
SWEEE
YES...
THAT'S IT...
NO!
BLAST!
THUMP!
HRMPH?
KNOCK
KNOCK
KNOCK
KNOCK
KNOCK
CLINK!

I WASN'T EXPECTING YOU SO SOON, KILL AUDIO.
GOTTA LEVEL WITH YOU, CLOCKLES. I DON'T THINK I KNEW HOW TOUGH THIS WAS GONNA BE.
I FIGURED SINCE YOU CONSTRUCTED ME WITH A SINGLE RESPONSIBILITY--
--I'D AT LEAST BE GOOD AT IT.
WHAT'S THAT?
OH, JUST DABBLING IN NEW LIFE FORMS.
PRACTICE MAKES PERFECT FOR ALL OF US. LET'S GET SOME AIR, SHALL WE?
TOK TIK TOK TIK TIK
SOMETHING HAS HAPPENED TO DISCOURAGE YOU, MY BOY?
YOU COULD SAY THAT. WHAT'S GETTING TO ME IS THAT THE GENRES WE'RE FINDING DON'T MAKE ANY SENSE.
THAT SOUNDS VERY STRANGE.
SKRATCH SKRATCH

ARE YOU EVEN PAYING ATTENTION?
IT'S NOT STRANGE. IT'S VERY METHODICAL.
AT ANY RATE, THE WAY THINGS ARE LOOKING, WE MAY AS WELL HAND MUSIC THE KEYS TO THE CITY.

!!
OH, DON'T BE SO DRAMATIC. YOU ARE MORE THAN EQUIPPED TO HANDLE THIS. I MADE YOU THAT WAY.

DRAMATIC? A FEW WEEKS AGO YOU WERE BLOWING A GASKET OVER THE SITUATION.
TIK
CLAK.
CLIK.
XXX
XXX

IF IT'S SO EASY ALL OF A SUDDEN, WHY DON'T YOU JUST GET MUSIC YOURSELF?

IT DOESN'T WORK LIKE THAT, KILL AUDIO. THE DAY YOU CAME BACK, THE BURDEN WAS NO LONGER MINE.
BOOF!

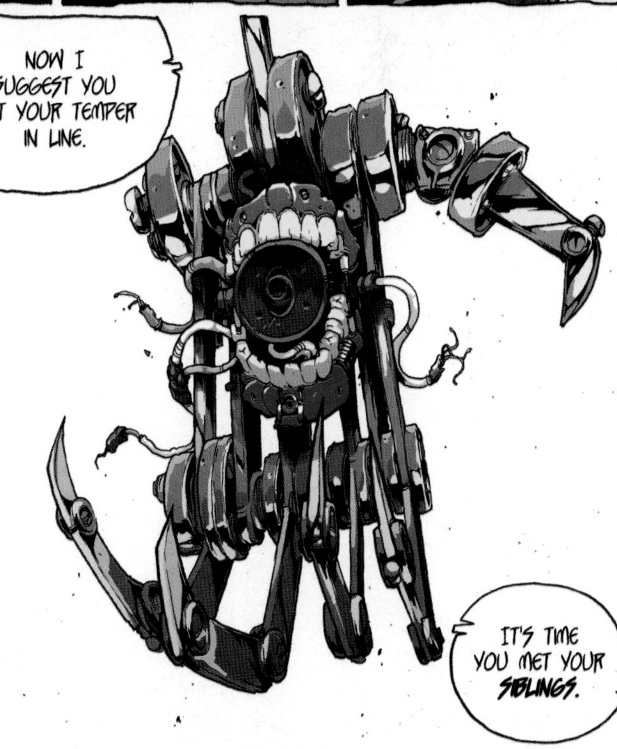
NOW I SUGGEST YOU GET YOUR TEMPER IN LINE.
IT'S TIME YOU MET YOUR SIBLINGS.

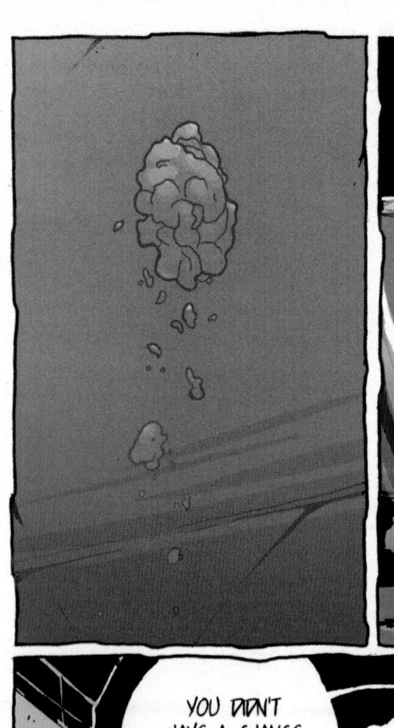

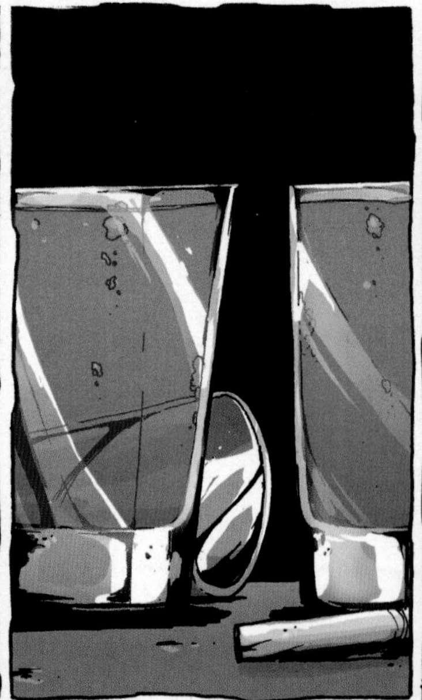

KLOK

YOU DIDN'T HAVE A CHANCE IN HELL.
DO YOU EVEN **HAVE** A LIVER?
I DON'T KNOW. I THINK I USED TO. WANNA TAKE A LOOK AND SEE?
NEWS

NEW

BLORR!
HEH HEH, LIGHT-WEIGHT.

SERIOUSLY THOUGH, MAYBE YOU SHOULD EASE UP UNTIL WE FIGURE OUT OUR GAME PLAN FOR TONIGHT.
NEWS
PSH
YOU PLAN THE GAME...

HEY!
GIVE IT BACK YOU BONEY RODENT BASTA--
CHUG.
CHUG.
CHUG *HIC*

SPLEEE
MFFA FFKKA!

THAT'S MORE LIKE IT.
CLARITY

WE DON'T HAVE TIME FOR HOMOEROTIC HUGS, BEAV. KA IS COUNTING ON US TO STRATEGIZE A WAY TO KEEP SURVEILLANCE ON JAZZ.

WE KNOW THAT JAZZ IS RUMORED TO OWN A CLUB CALLED THE BITCHES BREW. DO WE HAVE ANY MORE INFORMATION ON THE CLUB?
YOU'VE BEEN THERE BEFORE!
UMMMM...

RIGHT. WELL I REMEMBER THE DRINKS BEING VERY...STRONG. AND THERE WAS LIVE MUSIC.

SO IT FITS THE DESCRIPTION OF 99 PERCENT OF BARS IN SIGHT AND SOUND. YOU'VE GOT TO GIVE ME SOMETHING CHOOCH.
OK, SO I WAS WASTED. MOVING FORWARD.
IT'S PERTINENT WE GO THERE TONIGHT AND MAKE A FEW CONTACTS. SCOPE THE PLACE OUT. MAYBE SOMEONE HAS SEEN SOME OF THE OTHER FATHERS AROUND.
HIC

BRRRING!
BRRRRRINNG!
I GOT IT!
I GOT IT!
I GOT IT!
I GOT IT
HAH!
CLANG!
BOF
BONE ON THE PHONE. WHO'S THIS?
I'M LOOKING FOR MR. AUDIO. I HAVE SOME INFORMATION HE NEEDS TO HEAR.
IT'S A CHICK.
I CAN HEAR YOU MR. BONE. THIS IS IMPORTANT.
HEE HEE...
WANK WANK WANK
ON HER FACE
IT'S ABOUT THE WHERE-ABOUTS OF THE FATHERS.
WELL THEN I'LL HAVE TO TAKE A MESSAGE.
TELL HIM TO MEET ME AT MCPHAIL PARK AN HOUR AFTER SUNDOWN. YOU CAN'T MISS ME.

K-CHUK
OH
MY-
GOD!
IT'S POP!
REALLY!?
NO WAY!
OHMY GAWWD!
EEE!
SHRIIEEEK!!
EEE!
OH MY GOD, I LOVE YOU, POP!
SKRT
SKRT
SQUEEE
AAAH!

IN A RITZIER PART OF SIGHT AND SOUND.
SKYCAB01411
SO GOOD TO SEE YOU, BROTHER.
I THOUGHT WE'D GET RIGHT DOWN TO BUSINESS--
--BEFORE PLAYING DECADES WORTH OF CATCH UP.
--DRIVER, DOWNTOWN TO ALESEA, PLEASE--
KUMP
SOUNDS LIKE A PLAN TO ME.
TAKE A LOOK AROUND YOU, KILL. ANOTHER PRODUCTIVE DAY IN SIGHT AND SOUND--THE GEARS HARD AT WORK. BUT IT'S THE VOID WHO REALLY KEEP THIS CITY MOVING.
GLUG
ARE YOU IN CHARGE OF THIS PART OF TOWN TOO THEN?
THIS PART OF TOWN IS THE BUSINESS DISTRICT, MISTERIUM. THERE ISN'T A SPECIFIC VOID FOR INDUSTRY OR TECHNOLOGY BECAUSE THERE'S NO NEED.
EACH COG HERE KNOWS ITS ROLE AND WANTS NOTHING MORE THAN TO MAINTAIN THE PROVERBIAL MACHINE. IT'S THE ONES WHO THINK THEY'RE "ONE OF A KIND" THAT YOU NEED TO MONITOR.
SKYCAB01411

THE SELF-PROFESSED "ARTISTS" FLOCK TO ALESEA LIKE SHEEP. I'VE ALWAYS FOUND IT PECULIAR THAT THE MORE UNIQUE ONE FINDS HIMSELF TO BE, THE MORE HE NEEDS TO BE SURROUNDED BY THOSE HE FEELS ARE LIKE HIM.
SOMEWHAT OF A CONTRADICTION, DON'T YOU THINK? BUT THAT'S THE LIFE OF A DEMI.
SKRRRR
WHAT'S A DEMI?
CLOCKWORK DIDN'T TELL ME YOU WERE SO GREEN, KILL.
DEMI IS TAKEN FROM THE LATIN "DEMIURGE" MEANING ESSENTIALLY "LOCAL GOD."
THE VOID'S SLANG FOR THE CREATIVES AND THEIR NARCISSISTIC TENDENCIES.
SKRRCH
!
REEE
CHUNK
GOOD THING WE MET PRIOR TO OUR DINNER WITH WRIT AND DEMISE THIS EVENING. I'LL BRIEF YOU ON THE LINGO SO THEY DON'T MOCK YOU TO THE END OF TIME.
VMMMM
BEING THE BABY OF THE FAMILY IS BAD ENOUGH.

ROUGHLY ONE MINUTE EARLIER IN ALESEA.
TRY HARD
MISS! YOUR FORM IS EXQUISITE...I MUST PAINT YOU.
ANYTHING FOR THE SAKE OF ART!
FWIP!
SKRRT!
THIS WILL BE MY MOST EMBRYONIC PIECE TO DATE. RAW HUMAN FLESH COMBINED WITH ACRYLIC.
I'LL CALL IT "TWO-LEGGED SNAKE AND THE JACK OF ALL SPADES."

NOW.
WOW.
VRRRRMMMMMMm
YOU'RE LIKE THE KID WHO PISSED IN THE POOL.
I DIDN'T URINATE IN ANYONE'S SWIMMING POOL!
WASN'T BEING LITERAL, ART. I GUESS WE KNOW WHO GOT DEAR OLD DAD'S SENSE OF HUMOR. MAYBE I COULD TEACH YOU A FEW THINGS TOO.

MY VISION
IS A MENACE
TO THE EXISTENCE
OF THE ABSTRACT!
TAKE ME!
SLOSH!
NO MATTER HOW MANY TIMES I STOP TO SMELL THEM, I DON'T UNDERSTAND THE APPEAL OF THE ROSE.
SHOULD WE BE GOING AFTER THAT GUY?
IS THIS SOME KIND OF TEST YOU'RE THROWIN AT ME? WIZARD AND APPRENTICE TYPE NONSENSE?
AS INTERESTING AS THAT SOUNDS, THAT IS NOTHING MORE THAN AN EXAMPLE OF AN ORDINARY DEMI DESPERATE FOR RECOGNITION.
THE HUMAN CANVAS HAS BEEN A PART OF THE HISTORY BOOKS SINCE THE ABORIGINES WAR PAINT- FAR TOO TYPICAL TO BE A CAUSE FOR CONCERN.
QUITE UNLIKE WHAT WE HAVE OVER HERE...
DIB DAB
DO YOU HAVE THE TIME, PLEASE?
UM...I...
SOMETIMES DELIRIUM WHISPERS.

UH...
YOU SHOULD PUT SOMETHING ON THAT.
ALREADY DONE.
AT-YOUR SERVICE-MASTER.
DON'T-GET ANY-IDEAS.
NO!
MUTILATION IS--
--NOT WITHIN THE--
--GUIDELINES OF ART--
--WITHIN S&S!
IT'S A PERFORMANCE PIECE. YOU CAN'T HOLD US BACK FROM CREATING--
SHLOOP
SCOOP
--FOREVER.
HE SHOULD HAVE KNOWN I'D FIND HIM. *SIGH* DEMIS...
WELL, I THINK THAT'S ENOUGH ON THE JOB TRAINING FOR ONE DAY. LET ME ASK YOU THIS--
--DO YOU LIKE RED WINE?
SSCLICK

EARLIER THAT MORNING. WITHIN WHAT SOME MIGHT CALL A "FACTORY"–
LABOR MEANS VERY LITTLE TO MACHINES.
KZZZ
KSSS
VMMMM
VMMMMM
SOUND FEED
ORCHESTRATING THE SINGLE TONE TO END SIGHT AND SOUND HAS PROVEN TO REQUIRE MORE THAN ELECTRONICS. A CONDUCTOR NEEDS LIFE, ARDOR AND MOST IMPORTANTLY A RARE AMOUNT OF DEVOTION TO MUSIC ITSELF.
NOT A SOMETHING, BUT A SOMEONE.
IT'S THE LACK OF EMOTION THAT MADE THE ORIGINAL EQUIPMENT USELESS AS A CONDUCTOR.
TZZZZZ
ROCK
SOUND FEED
BEGIN COMPOSITION OF MULTI-GENRE SYMPHONY.

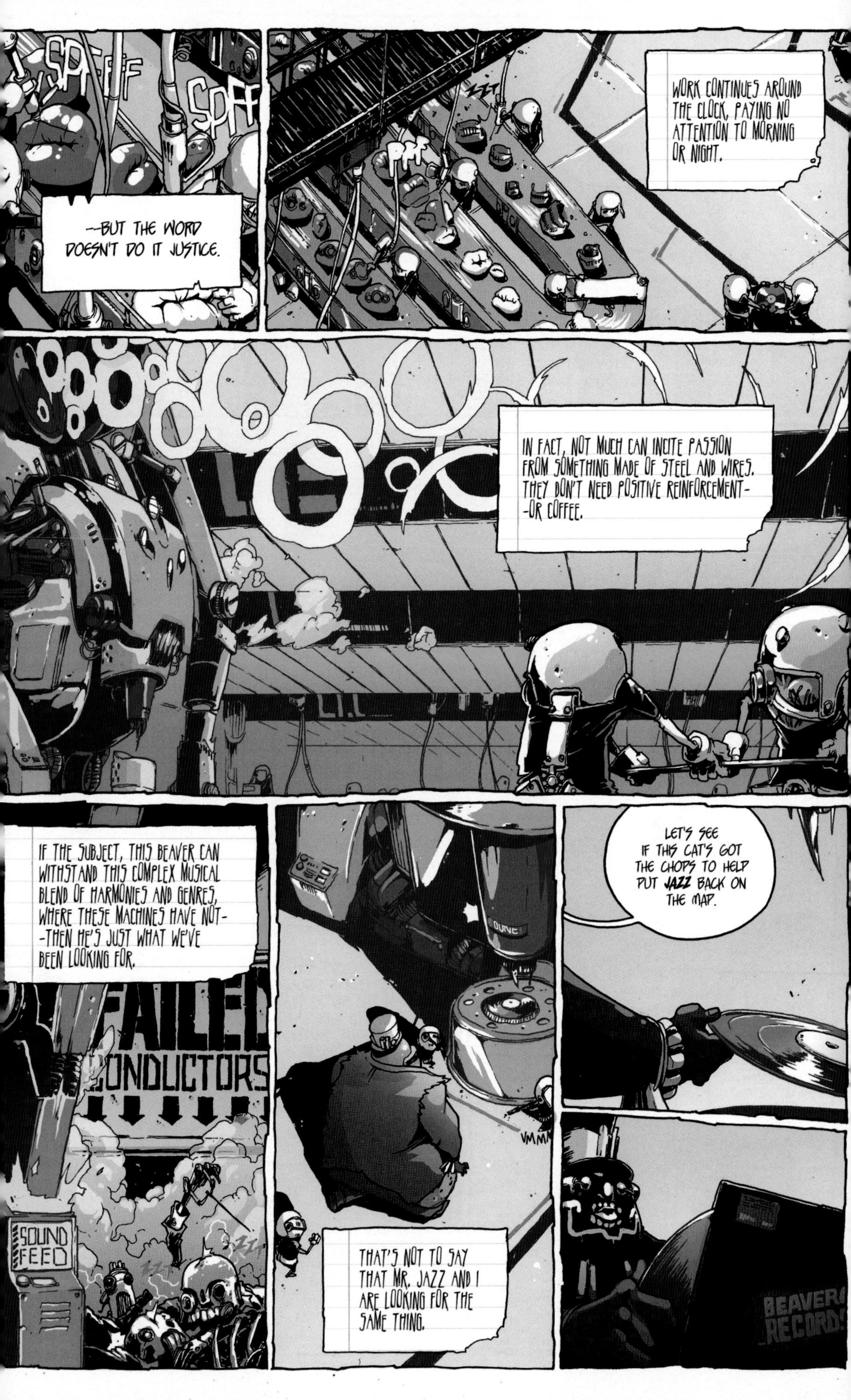
SPFFF
SPFF
--BUT THE WORD DOESN'T DO IT JUSTICE.
PFF
WORK CONTINUES AROUND THE CLOCK, PAYING NO ATTENTION TO MORNING OR NIGHT.
IN FACT, NOT MUCH CAN INCITE PASSION FROM SOMETHING MADE OF STEEL AND WIRES. THEY DON'T NEED POSITIVE REINFORCEMENT--OR COFFEE.
IF THE SUBJECT, THIS BEAVER CAN WITHSTAND THIS COMPLEX MUSICAL BLEND OF HARMONIES AND GENRES, WHERE THESE MACHINES HAVE NOT--THEN HE'S JUST WHAT WE'VE BEEN LOOKING FOR.
FAILED CONDUCTORS
SOUND FEED
VMMM
THAT'S NOT TO SAY THAT MR. JAZZ AND I ARE LOOKING FOR THE SAME THING.
LET'S SEE IF THIS CAT'S GOT THE CHOPS TO HELP PUT JAZZ BACK ON THE MAP.
BEAVER RECORDS

THIS WINE TASTES GOOD. LIKE FRUITS.

IT DOES HAVE EXCELLENT NOTES OF PLUM...

CLINK

DINK

TINK

HOW LOVELY TO HAVE YOU BACK WITH US, KILL. WHAT HAVE YOU BEEN DOING WITH YOURSELF ALL THESE YEARS?

HOW ABOUT DESSERT?
THEY'VE ALWAYS BEEN AN UNRULY BUNCH. NOT LIKE MY THESPIANS. AND TO BE BROUGHT UP WITH NO DISCIPLINE CERTAINLY HASN'T HELPED.
YOU ASK THEM GENRES WHEN YOU GET THEM? THEY COULD KNOW A LOT OF INFORMATION ABOUT THE HIDING PLACE.
TERRIBLE IDEA! NO ONE WILL TALK. I'D VENTURE TO SAY THEY MIGHT EVEN TAKE PRIDE IN DYING FOR A CAUSE. CREATIVITY IS NOT WHAT IT USED TO BE.
EVERYDAY I SEE THE LINES BECOME A LITTLE MORE BLURRED. ARTISTS BEGGING TO BE CAUGHT TO PROVE A POINT. BEING A DANGER TO THE WORLD OF CREATION INTRIGUES THEM IN THE WAY IT USED TO FRIGHTEN THEM.
I DON'T THINK THAT'S THE CASE FOR ALL OF US. THE WORLD OF THEATER IS PASSIVE AS ALWAYS--
--AND I'M LUCKY TO BE GETTING THE WRITERS TO COME AWAY FROM THEIR MINDS LONG ENOUGH TO DO BAD THINGS.

IF ONE OF US IS AFFECTED, WE ARE ALL AT RISK. IF ART CONTINUES TO TEST ITS LIMITS BY NEGLECTING MEDIUMS FOR THE ACT OF CREATION ITSELF-
RUM
TSS
-WHO'S TO SAY IT WON'T GROW TO ENCOMPASS EVERYTHING? EVEN THAT IT OPPOSES?
CLOCKWORK WOULD NEVER ALLOW THAT TO HAPPEN.
NOW LET'S STOP TURNING THIS DINNER PARTY INTO YOUR PERSONAL PREDICTION OF ARMAGEDDON AND GET BACK TO KILL'S PREDICAMENT.
RING!
OF COURSE. HE'S RIGHT HERE.
KILL, YOU HAVE A CALL.
YEAH?
I'LL BE THERE AS SOON AS I CAN.

McPHAIL PARK

CHUK
KCHUK
SKRCH

DO YOU KNOW WHAT **INCONSPICUOUS** MEANS?
I THINK THE SPEEDOMETER IS BROKEN.

SWEET MOTHER OF-
YOU MUST BE--
--WELL I NEVER GOT YOUR NAME, ACTUALLY.
MY-
NAME-
IS-
-HEAVY METAL.

TSK
BEAV SAID IT WAS A LADY ON THE PHONE.
IT WAS A LADY ON THE PHONE.
I'VE LEARNED IF YOU WANT SOMETHING DONE, YOU GOTTA TAKE THE REINS.
SO I CAME TO TELL YOU MYSELF-
-WE RE NOT AMUSED BY YOUR RETURN.
TSK
YOU THOUGHT YOU HAD YOURSELF A LITTLE SNITCH, HUH?
SOMEONE TO BOTTLE FEED YOU INFORMATION ABOUT US?
SOMEONE NEEDS TO TEACH YOU WHO RUNS THINGS AROUND HERE.
POOM
TOK
I HATE ELTON JOHN.
COOL YOUR JETS, BENNIE. MAYBE THIS WILL ENTERTAIN YOU.
BLAM
BLAM

BOOF
DONK
WHAT KIND OF SH--
-AAARGH!!
NYEH HEH HEE!
CHCK
RAR!
CHCHAK
RRRA!
IF YOU CAN'T BEAT 'EM--
CHK-CHUK
--JOIN 'EM.

CHAPTER 4

THE SOUTHWESTERN OUTSKIRTS OF SIGHT AND SOUND--
OOOU.
--WHERE THE DEER AND THE ANTELOPE PLAY.
UNF.
TAA
TAT
TA
BUT THIS IS NO TYPICAL DAY ON THE RANGE.
PA! UNCLE ALT!
TP
TP
TP
PAAA!!
HAF.
HUF.
GRANDMAMMY... FOLK'S...
HUF.
GONE... MISSIN'!

178 XXX AVE.
APT.22. SOUTH MELODIA,
SIGHT & SOUND
BEAVER RECORDS
?
?
"BEAVER RECORDS"?
HMMM--
--YES! IT MUST BE A SUBMISSION FOR MY RECORD LABEL.
BUT YOU DON'T HAVE ONE.
SNATCH
BVOORR
WHAT THE HELL DO YOU KNOW? I DO HAVE A LABEL AND AM IN THE PROCESS OF FINDING THE NEXT ZEPPELIN. I DON'T HAVE TO TELL YOU EVERYTHING.
IT'S LIKE NAILS ON A CHALKBOARD HAD A LOVE CHILD WITH A TONE-DEAF SEAGULL.
HANDS DOWN THE MOST HORRIBLE SONG I HAVE EVER HEARD.
YOU'VE GOT TO BE KIDDING ME.
THIS JAM IS AWESOME-
--AND I'M SIGNING THIS BAND.

BENEATH SIGHT AND SOUND.
NNM- -NMF!
NFF!!
NMM!
MM
NMF!!
NO NEED TO STRUGGLE, MY DEAR--
NM!!
MM!!
TSSSSSSS

THER OF CLASSICAL 01
FATHER OF CLASSICAL 01
FATHER OF OLK

FATHER OF ROCK 02
FATHER OF ROCK 02
--ALL YOUR FRIENDS ARE ALREADY HERE.
FATHER OF ELECTRO 04

GET YOU GUYS ANOTHER ROUND A' JITTERSAUCE?.
THREE WHISKEYS HERE AND A SELTZER FOR THE PAPER. HE'S ON THE JOB.
SURE THING BOSS. WE GOT LIVE MUSIC COMING UP ANY MINUTE-
-A DOWNRIGHT CANARY IF YOU ASK ME.
IN THAT CASE, I BETTER BLOW A LITTLE MYSELF.
SO BRIEF ME ON WHAT WE'RE DOING HERE GUYS. YOU KNOW I CAN'T FUNCTION WITHOUT A REASON.
JUST BE READY TO REPEAT THE ASS KICKING WE SAW YOU GIVE HEAVY METAL AND WE'LL BE GLAD TO HAVE YOU AROUND.
ALSO, KEEP YOUR EYES PEELED FOR ANYTHING OUT OF THE ORDINARY.
UM, LIKE HER?
SNRRK
GOOD EVENING, GENTLEMEN.
YEAH!
AWOOO
MAMA!
OW!
AWEEE
OH!
IT'S GREAT TO BE HERE AT THE BITCHES BREW. THIS SONG IS ABOUT FALLING IN LOVE--
--WITH A LECHEROUS FRAUD OF A MAMA'S BOY WHO SUCKS YOUR SOUL DRY. IT'S CALLED "CUT THE CORD."

YO, LITTLE MAN, IT'S YOUR CHICK! THE ONE FROM THE FOREST.
AHEH-HEM...
THUNK
THUNK
THUNK
THANKS, CAPTAIN OBVIOUS.
I KISSED A LOT OF FROGS
THEN I MADE OUT WITH A FRAUD
YOU GUYS ARE GREAT. GONNA TAKE 5.
THUD

AND I THOUGHT THE SCOTCH WAS THE SMOOTHEST THING AT THIS BAR.

IN HONOR OF AN UNEXPECTED REUNION, I'LL LET YOU BUY ME A DRINK.

HELL, I'LL BUY YOU **TWO.**

EXIT

WONDER WHY IT'S SO DEAD IN HERE TONIGHT?

THE POINT BEING--
ROCK
JAZZ
CLASS
--IF THIS JAZZ CHARACTER'S THE TALK OF THE TOWN, HOW COME HE'S WITHOUT AN ENTOURAGE SUPPORTING HIS ESTABLISHMENT?
ARE YOU WRITING THIS DOWN?
BEEP! BEEP!
HM?
DAMN, CHOOCH. YOU'RE USELESS!
IS THAT A BOOBIE?
I DON'T KNOW, I'VE NEVER SEEN ONE.
BEEP! BEEP!
I WAS PROMISED LIVE MUSIC.
GOOD THING I BROUGHT BACKUP.
YOUR "MUSIC" JUST TOOK KA INTO THAT DARK CORNER.
I'M GONNA CALL IT A NIGHT GUYS. GOT SOME BIZ TO HANDLE.
BEEP! BEEP!
PHASE 1
HE LOVES IT. WE GOT A WINNER.
HE'S BEEN LISTENING TO THIS GARBAGE ALL DAY.

SO WHY'D YOU LEAVE THE TORRENT GATES?
WELL, LURING TRESPASSERS TO THEIR DEATHS WASN'T NEARLY AS MUCH FUN ALL BY MYSELF, SO I MOVED TO THE CITY. WHEN I MENTIONED MY PAST EXPERIENCE AS A SIREN, JAZZ OFFERED ME THIS GIG.
I CAN TRY OUT NEW MATERIAL AND WHEN THE PATRONS SNAP OUT OF IT, THEY'RE SOBER ENOUGH FOR ANOTHER ROUND.
KIND OF A WIN-WIN SITUATION.
SOUNDS LIKE THINGS ARE GOING BETTER ON YOUR END THAN MINE. I'M STARTING TO THINK I WAS BETTER OFF NOT KNOWING ANYTHING ABOUT MYSELF.
IT FIGURES THAT YOU TURN OUT TO BE THE ABSENCE OF MUSIC.
KINDA TAKES MY LOVE OF UNHEALTHY RELATIONSHIPS TO A NEW LEVEL.
HOW DID YOU KNOW I'M A VOID?
SINCE THAT SQUEAKY FRIEND OF YOURS STUMBLED IN HERE, YOUR NAME GETS THROWN AROUND ALL THE TIME.
FOLK IS THE ONLY FATHER WHO'S BEEN IN HERE FOR MONTHS AND A LOT OF THE SUB-GENRES HAVE BEEN FINDING NEW PLACES TO DRINK.
JAZZ THINKS YOUR RETURN COULD DESTROY EVERYTHING HE'S WORKED FOR.
OUT FRONT
SKRCH
KLAK
CLOP
TIME FOR THIS ROCK TO ROLL...

I AIN'T WEARIN' MY CRAP KICKERS FER NOTHING--
--WE CAME TO SETTLE SOME HASH WITH JAZZ.
SLAM
SHING
YA'LL IN HERE PAINTIN' YER TONSILS WITH COFFIN VARNISH WHILE OUR MAMA COULD BE ANYPLACE ON SIGHT AND SOUND.
NOW SOMEBODY KNOWS SOMETHIN'. QUIT TRYIN' T'SAVE YER BACON--
EEK!
OH MY!
SHH!
--OR MS. BLACK-EYED SUSAN HERE'LL HAVE TO TALK FOR YA.
WHAT SEEMS TO BE THE TROUBLE, BOYS?
CH-LUK

--SHUT YER MOUTHS WITH THE SNIPSNAP.

WHERE IS HE?

GUP!

HARM ONE HAIR ON ***EITHER*** OF THOSE HEADS AND I'LL MAKE SURE YOUR MOMMY ***DOESN'T COME HOME.***

!?

!?

SNAKES ALIVE, IF IT'S NOT THAT SCALAWAG FROM THE VOID. MIND IF I ASK WHAT YER DOIN' PATRONIZIN' THE 'STABLISHMENT OF A FATHER?
THE SAME REASON YOU ARE. JAZZ. NOW LEAVE THE LADY ALONE.
YOU'RE SWEET ON HER?
HOLD UP JUST A SECON'--
--MY POWERS OF DEDUCTIVE REASONIN' TELL ME IF YOU'RE HERE TO TAKE AWAY JAZZ, MAYBE HE'S GOT NOTHIN' TO DO WITH MAMA AND IT'S YOU WE WANT AFTER ALL.
I'M HERE TO TALK WITH HIM ABOUT THE MISSING FATHERS.
YA SAYIN' YA'LL ARE IN CAHOOTS, THEN?
WHAT I'M SAYING WESTERN WEAR, IS GET YOUR HANDS OFF MY GIRL.
I WON'T ASK YOU AGAIN.
HOWEVER YA SPIN IT, YOU HAD A HAND IN TAKIN' OUR MAMA, SO WE'RE TAKIN' CALAMITY JANE HERE.
TIT FOR TAT.

HOPE YOU CAN COOK.
YA'LL STAY PUT NOW, AND NOBODY GETS HU--
OOF!
TRIP!
TARNATION!
KILL!!
MOTHER CLUCKER!!
RAA!
SPUTZ!
--ALL TH
FIGHTIN'S
MAKIN' M
HUNGRY!
CHICKENS, VARMINTS--
HEY, CLETUS!

!?
SPTOO
DINNER'S READY!!
GAH!
THAT'S ENOUGH!!
YA'LL BETTER HEED ME NOW...
I CAN EITHER PLUG THE FOUR OF YOU WITH THE FIVE BULLETS I GOT LEFT...
OR I CAN POP 'EM ALL INTO THIS CHERRY SPITTER RIGHT HERE! NOW--
SNAP
!?
WE COULD HAVE DONE THIS WITH A LITTLE MORE CIVILITY.
GROSS.
BUT SINCE YOU'D RATHER SETTLE THINGS DIRTY, I'LL BE HAPPY TO OBLIGE--
--YEE-HAW.

AFTERWARDS, ON THE WAY HOME.
JAZZ LEFT IN A HURRY. FROM MY EXPERIENCE, INNOCENT MEN NEVER FLEE THE SCENE.
BUK-BUK-BU BUCOCK!
EXACTLY. BUT THAT PLACE IS HIS LIVELIHOOD. I GUARANTEE HE WON'T STAY AWAY LONG.
DOES THAT MEAN WE HAVE TO SPEND ANOTHER NIGHT AT THE BAR?
CAN'T WE GO PAINTBALLING OR SOMETHING?
COCK-A-DOODLE DOOOOO, BABY!
WE CAN DO FUN THINGS TO YOUR HEART'S CONTENT DJ--
BEEP! BEEP!
--AFTER WE GET TO THE BOTTOM OF JAZZ'S INVOLVEMENT IN THE FATHERS' DISAPPEARANCES.
APPROACHING RESIDENCE. PHASE TWO.
FT FTTR

WHAT A DAY!
FLICK!
NO DEEP CUTS TONIGHT, THIS BONE'S DRY.
ME TOO. NEED...SLEEP...
YOU TWO LOVEBIRDS CARE TO WATCH A MOVIE? I HAVE ALL THE CLASSICS!
I'M PRETTY TIRED ACTUALLY. MAYBE IN THE MORNING?
YAWN!
EAT 'EM
SIGH.
HEY FEATHERS, LEMME GET IN ON A LITTLE CINEMATIC ACTION WITH YA.
YOU'LL BE INTERESTED TO KNOW THAT RAY PARKER JR. WROTE THIS THEME SONG, THOUGH BEAV AND HUEY LEWIS WOULD BEG TO DIFFER. I READ AN INTERVIEW CLAIMING HE WAS INSPIRED BY THE LINE "WHO YOU GONNA CALL" FROM A DRAIN COMPANY COMMERCIAL.
MY FAVORITE'S VENKMEN. BEAV HAS A THING FOR JANINE. WHO'S YOURS?
PLEASE DO!
SNORRR!!
MAN...

SNORR

♥

Z.

YAWN.

BEEP!
BEEP!

ONE TALL ICED CHAI. LOWFAT MILK.
PSHHH
SIGH ...THANKS.
...
IF YOU'RE INTERESTED IN ANY OF THOSE, ALL THE ARTWORK IS FOR SALE.
YOU'RE KIDDING RIGHT? THERE'S NOTHING IN THOSE FRAMES.
THE PAINTINGS REFLECT THE PATTERN OF THE WALLPAPER, CREATING A SENSE OF UNITY.
MAYBE YOU JUST DON'T GET THE IRONY.
GUESS NOT.
SIGH

UGH, THIS SOY MOCHA LATTE TASTES LIKE DIRT. DID THAT BARISTA ASK YOU FOR YOUR AUTOGRAPH?
NO, SHE TRIED TO SELL ME CRAPPY ARTWORK.
I JUST DON'T UNDERSTAND WHAT HAPPENED TO CELEBRITY. HOW DO WE GET FAMOUS WHEN NO ONE CARES?
I HAVE A SURPRISE FOR EVERYONE.
SURPRISE!
OH, WHAT ARE **THOSE?**
SOMETHIN' I PICKED UP DOWNTOWN. A JAZZY LITTLE BIRDIE TOLD ME THEY'RE THE FAST TRACK TO **STARDOM.**
♪
ALL WE HAVE TO DO IS HAND THEM OUT AROUND TOWN AND THESE **KISSERS** ARE GONNA GET US HEARD.
OVER AND **OVER.**
♪

A FEW STOREFRONTS DOWN IN ***ALESEA.***

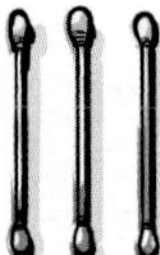

I CAN'T SAY I UNDERSTAND IT--

--BUT THEY SAY ART IS SUBJECTIVE.

THE FLOWERS TAKE CENTER STAGE, DON'T THEY?

AMAZING THEY WERE ABLE TO ACQUIRE SO MANY OF SUCH A RARE VARIETY.

EAR CLEANING ISN'T FOR ART SHOW.

WELL HOW ABOUT THIS PIECE CALLED ***"SCEPTER OF THE UNIVERSE"?*** THE SIMPLICITY IS ***ASTOUNDING!***

THERE'S NO DEEP STATEMENT BEHIND IT. IT'S ALMOST NOT LIKE ART AT ALL.

WELL I'M SURE IT'S JUST A PHASE IN THE DEMI COMMUNITY. MIGHT AS WELL ENJOY IT WHILE IT LASTS.
FOR THE FIRST TIME IN MY LIFE, I CERTAINLY AM.
SHUT THAT THING OFF ALREADY!
RIIING
IT'S TRULY TASTELESS TO HAVE A CELL PHONE IN A GALLERY.
THAT IS YOUR PHONE!
OH! PARDON ME.
MURDER, HERE.
ART, I DIDN'T KNOW WHO ELSE TO CALL-
--ONE OF MY CREW--
--BEAV IS MISSING.
TO BE CONTINUED...

CHAPTER 5

STAND CLEAR
PSH
WELL... WHAT DO WE DO NOW?
WE GO OUT AND MAKE SOME NOISE.
DOES ANYONE KNOW WHERE WE ARE?
I HAVE NO IDEA.
PROMOTIONAL MATERIAL
BUT I HOPE THERE'S A MUSIC SHOP CLOSE BY.
SUB-GENRES GENERATOR
EXIT ONLY
DUMP
FOLK ROCK CLASS. ELEC

RESTRICTED ARE
GOOD AFTERNOON!
NOTHING GOOD ABOUT IT, HAMMERNOSE!
YOU'VE HAD ME IN HERE FOR LORD KNOWS HOW LONG AND I HAVEN'T HAD A SINGLE CIGARETTE. BESIDES BEING A TRAITOR BASTARD, YOU'VE PERFECTED THE ART OF TORTURE.
RNK
RLNK
RAKL
I CAN FIX THAT--
--AND FOR THE RECORD, THE PURPOSE ISN'T TO TORTURE YOU.
SWIP
CLOP
SSSSP!
OH IT'S NOT? YOU'VE GOT THE FATHERS BOLTED TO SOME MACHINE LIKE A BUNCH OF VEALS--

--YOU TORE ME OUT OF THE BEAVER DAM IN THE WEE HOURS, WHICH NO LIVING MAN HAS EVER SUCCESSFULLY ATTEMPTED.
AND NOW I'M STRAPPED DOWN WITHOUT ACCESS TO MY TUNES. CUSTOMER SERVICE DOESN'T SEEM LIKE A STRONG POINT AROUND HERE.
YOU AREN'T A PRISONER, MR. BEAVER--
YOU'RE AN HONORED GUEST. I DON'T KNOW IF YOU'VE NOTICED, BUT THE WORLD IS BROKEN.
I'VE LIVED IN THIS WORLD A LOT LONGER THAN YOU AND IT SEEMS FINE TO ME.
I NEVER WOULD'VE SEEN THE LIGHT EITHER IF HE HADN'T POINTED IT OUT. I'D STILL BE BUSY CORRECTING INSIGNIFICANT THINGS.
BUT HE GAVE ME THE CHANCE TO BE A PART OF THE BIGGEST REPAIR JOB SIGHT AND SOUND WILL EVER SEE.
SNAK
SNIK
AS LONG AS CREATIVITY CONTINUES ON THIS SCREWED UP PATH, THERE WILL BE MISTAKES.
SNIK
ALWAYS SOMETHING TO FIX.
I'M NOT CONTENT TO KEEP LIVING WITHOUT AN END IN SIGHT TO THE CONSTANT CORRECTIONS. THIS JOB IS KILLING ME. I NEED PEACE.
SNAK
AND YOU CAN'T TELL ME YOU'RE PROUD OF THE STATE OF MUSIC, MR. BEAVER. I'M NOT SUGGESTING YOU TURN YOUR BACK ON WHAT YOU LOVE.
AFTER TONIGHT'S DELIVERY, MOVE THEM TO CONCERT MODE.
ROGER THAT.
ALL HE'S ASKING US TO DO IS HELP GIVE IT A CLEAN SLATE.
YOU SHOULD REALLY THINK ABOUT WHAT SIDE YOU'RE ON.

CLOSING TIME AT THE BITCHES BREW.
OPEN
CLOSED
GO HOME DAMMIT
I'M FEELIN' GENEROUS. WHY DON'T YOU GET ON OUT OF HERE A LITTLE EARLY TONIGHT, FRANKIE?
RELEASE OF TENSION UNKNOWN...
SHOO
REALLY? THANKS BOSS!
I'M NOT GETTIN' SOFT. HURRY UP BEFORE I CHANGE MY MIND.
...MIND WORKS THE FINGERS TO THE BONE...
...I WON'T PRAY FOR YOU...
...BITCHES BREW, HOW'D YOU KNOW...
SKEE
BITCHES BREW, HOW'D YOU KNOW I WON'T PRAY FOR YOU?

PRAY FOR TIME TO SET YOU FREE...
SHLUP
YOUR MOTHER DID WARN YOU FROM INSIDE...
SWOOF
NOW YOU'RE BACK ON DRY LAND...
OOF!
PUMF
CURSE THE PLACE WHERE I STAND
KLAK
BAH!
C'MERE YOU TRICKY, SUMBITCH--
SINCE WHEN DID THE OWNER DO THE DIRTY WORK AROUND HERE?
WHAT THE--
DAMN, MAN! ALMOST GAVE ME A HEART ATTACK. WHAT BRINGS YOU A'KNOCKIN AT THIS HOUR, JACK?
HOPE IT'S THE NEWS I'VE BEEN WAITIN' FOR!

THE CONDUCTOR IS FINALLY IN CUSTODY AND WE'VE BEGUN MOVING FORWARD.
BUT AS I WAS GETTING EVERY-THING IN ORDER, I REALIZED I'M MISSING A KEY SOUND COMPONENT--
--THE FINAL FATHER.
WAIT A SECOND HERE. THAT BEAVER WAS SUPPOSED TO INCREASE PRODUCTION SO WE COULD SPEED UP MY DEBUT BROADCAST. YOU AGREED IT WAS TIME FOR JAZZ TO TAKE BACK THE MUSICAL THRONE!
WE HAD A DEAL.
PERHAPS I SHOULD ASK YOUR FELLOW FATHERS HOW MUCH DEALS APPEAR TO MEAN AROUND HERE. I'M SURE YOU HAVEN'T FORGOTTEN THE CODE YOU SIGNED WITH THEM AT THE BEGINNING OF SIGHT AND SOUND. THE PLEDGE TO PROTECT EACH OTHER'S INTERESTS AS YOUR OWN?
RUMOR HAS IT COUNTRY WAS IN HERE RECENTLY TO REMIND YOU OF THAT BETRAYAL.
YOU FILTHY SON'OF'A--
=BFF!
--SPARE ME, JAZZ. I'VE JUST LEARNED TO MASTER BEAUTY.
AARGH!
EXIT
I CAN'T POSSIBLY GRASP THE CONCEPT OF LOYALTY YET.

HOOONK
HOOOONK
KNT
SKRT T T

VMM
SKRCH

WHOEVER THAT WAS LEFT IN A HURRY. LET'S HAVE A LOOK AROUND.
HOPE IT WASN'T WHO WE'RE LOOKING FOR, BABY!
YEAH, I COULDN'T HANDLE COMING BACK HERE AGAIN.

DIDN'T EVEN GET A CHANCE TO FINISH THEIR BOURBON.

IF ANYONE'S HERE, YOU BETTER LISTEN UP!

I'M NOT LEAVING THIS PLACE UNTIL YOU GIVE ME BACK MY FRIEND!
PLOP

SORRY BUDDY, THE BREW LOOKS EMPTY. MAYBE THAT CAR THAT JUST PEELED OUT GOT TO JAZZ BEFORE WE DID.
WHAT ABOUT BEAV THEN? WHERE'S A BROTHER GO WHEN HIS KIDNAPPER IS KIDNAPPED?

NEWS
WE'RE NEVER GONNA FIND HIM. JUST LEAVE ME HERE. I CAN'T GO ON ALONE.
WHAT'S THIS?

THANK YOU FOR SEEING US ON SUCH SHORT NOTICE.
SORRY THE PLACE IS A DISASTER. WE'VE BEEN SO FOCUSED ON FINDING BEAV...
YOU HAVEN'T NO LUCK WITH THAT?
NOT YET. BUT AS SOON AS WE'RE FINISHED HERE, I'M MEETING UP WITH THE GANG AT JAZZ'S BAR TO QUESTION THAT SONUVABITCH.
COUNTRY SEEMED TO THINK HE HAD SOMETHING TO DO WITH THE FATHERS, SO I DON'T KNOW WHAT HE'S CAPABLE OF.
I THINK THAT'S AN EXCELLENT PLACE TO START.
NOW, I KNOW YOU'RE IN A HURRY, BUT THIS WILL ONLY TAKE A MOMENT.
IT PAINS ME DEEPLY TO SAY THIS, KILL, BUT OUR BROTHER, ART, SEEMS TO BE... **MALFUNCTIONING**.

WAIT, THAT CAN HAPPEN? ARE YOU TRYING TO TELL ME WE'RE ROBOTS? HELL OF A BOMBSHELL AT A TIME LIKE THIS.
NO, NO, OF COURSE NOT. BUT HE'S BEEN ACTING TERRIBLY BIZARRE. CERTAINLY NOT CHARACTERISTIC OF A MEMBER OF THE VOID.
OK. NOT TO RUSH YOU--
--THIS JUST SOUNDS LIKE A CONVERSATION FOR CLOCKWORK. I GET THAT YOU'RE CONCERNED--
--BUT I'VE GOTTA GO LOOK FOR MY FRIEND. THE CLOCK'S TICKING. NO PUN INTENDED.
TRY HARDER TO UNDERSTANDING.
AT THE ALESEA GALLERY OPEN, ART TOOK SOMETHING TO HIS HOME. HE PAID THE DOLLARS FOR IT!

...
COME AGAIN?
CLEARLY THERE'S AN ISSUE DEMISE, BUT I'M SURE IT'S NOTHING CLOCK-WORK CAN'T--
IF CLOCKWORK FINDS OUT, HE'LL DESTROY ART AND CREATE A NEW MODERATOR. CLOCKWORK ISN'T CRUEL, BUT AS YOU KNOW, TIME IS OF THE ESSENCE WITH HIM.
THE ABSENCE OF ART HIMSELF PURCHASED A PIECE FROM AN ART EXHIBIT. WHY WOULD HE DO THAT?
RRR...
WRIT AND I THINK WE SHOULD CONFRONT THE SITUATION FIRST. MAKE SURE HE'S OK. WE ARE A FAMILY AFTER ALL.
I THOUGHT YOU'D AGREE.
I DO BUT--
--SOMETHING'S VERY WRONG, KILL.

HELLO!?
WHOSE CAR IS THAT?
IS HE BACK?!
NOT YET, DJ. THIS IS MY BROTHER AND SISTER.
NICE TO MEET YOU.
WHY ARE YOU GUYS BACK SO SOON? WHERE'S JAZZ?
IT SEEMS LIKE SOMEONE ELSE WANTED HIM TOO. THAT PLACE WAS WIDER OPEN THAN A WHORE HOUSE ON VALENTINE'S DAY.
IT'S ONLY STRIKE TWO. HEY, YOU MIND GIVING ME AOD FOR A MINUTE? ME AND CHI-CO WANT TO REVIEW SOME OF THE CAPTURES.
THIS MIGHT BE AS SIMPLE AS A SUB LOOKING FOR VENGEANCE.
SIGH
NEWS

THAT'D BE A GREAT SURPRISE.
PLEASE. DON'T-SEND ME-WITH-THE SIMPLETONS.
YOU'LL BE FINE.
TRY TO KEEP HIS ATTITUDE UNDER CONTROL.
DON'T WORRY, WE'LL MAKE SURE THE BELT STAYS DEMORALIZED.
NEWS
WHEN-WAS THE-LAST-TIME YOU-WASHED YOUR-HANDS!?
TAKE CARE, BABIES! PLEASURE FINALLY MEETING LITTLE MAN'S FAMILY TIES.
PLEASURE TO MEET TOO COCK!
PLEASE ACCEPT MY SYMPATHY FOR YOUR FRIEND. I'M SURE HE'LL TURN UP.
WHAT DO YOU HAVE THERE?
AH, SOME FLOWER PETAL I FOUND. IT SMELLS NICE.
SUCH A BEAUTIFUL FLOWER, THE CHERYLIAN ROSE.
AND VERY DIFFICULT TO CULTIVATE. OUR BROTHER ART'S GARDENER HAS JUST GOTTEN THE HANG OF GROWING THEM.

BUT ART HATES ROSES. HE SAID IT IN ALESEA.
HATED ROSES. IT'S ANOTHER ONE OF HIS NEWFOUND INTERESTS.
DJ, WHERE DID YOU FIND THIS PETAL?
AT THE BITCHES BREW.
HOLY FATHERS...
...I THINK OUR BROTHER'S RESPONSIBLE FOR DESTROYING MUSIC.

CONCERT ROOM
DING
I'D LIKE TO THANK YOU ALL FOR COMING TONIGHT.

SURE, SOME MIGHT ARGUE YOU DIDN'T HAVE A CHOICE, BUT THAT WOULD BE INCORRECT. IN FACT, IT'S EACH ONE OF OUR CHOICES THAT HAVE LED US HERE--
--MILLIONS OF BABY STEPS STRAIGHT TO THIS DESTINY.
TAKE ME FOR EXAMPLE. NONE OF YOU COULD POSSIBLY UNDERSTAND WHAT IT'S LIKE TO BE VOID OF CREATIVITY. TO NEVER BE ABLE TO EXPRESS YOURSELF.
DOOP
CHARGE
WELL I COULDN'T UNDERSTAND IT EITHER.
KILL'S DISAPPEARANCE WAS A BLESSING IN DISGUISE. WITHOUT HIM HERE TO BABY SIT ALL OF YOU, I COULD TRY MY HAND AT INVENTING NEW GENRES RIGHT IN THIS ROOM.
SO MANY YEARS OF BEING TOLD I WAS STERILE, ONLY TO BIRTH THOUSANDS OF CHILDREN.
MEANWHILE, THE MINIMALIST TREND IN THE ART WORLD BEGAN TO CHANGE MY VOID.
WHAT WAS ONCE FLAMBOYANT BECAME ORDINARY.
IT BECAME ME. THE ANTI-ART.
THAT'S WHEN I REALIZED THIS WHOLE WORLD WAS FLAWED. AND I VISUALIZED BIGGER DREAMS THAN APPREHENDING ARTISTS AND COMPOSING SILLY MUSICAL HALF-BREEDS.
SHLP

I SAW OPPORTUNITY TO LIVE UP TO MY FULL POTENTIAL AND GIVE EVERYONE IN SIGHT AND SOUND THE PRETTIEST PAINTING OF ALL TIME.
A FRESH CANVAS WE COULD WORK ON TOGETHER, WHERE CREATIVITY FLOWS FREELY AND IS WITHHELD FROM NO ONE.
SHWAAAAH
BUT I CAN'T TAKE ALL THE CREDIT.
SOME SHOULD GO TO YOUR DEAR BROTHER, JAZZ, WHO IN BETRAYING HIS OWN FAMILY, FURTHER PROVED THE DISGRACE OF THIS SYSTEM.
HIS DESPERATION FOR FAME MADE HIM A PERFECT CANDIDATE TO INFILTRATE THE CITY WITH THE MOUTHPIECES. HE HAD EVERY GENRE IN S & S SPREADING THEM ACROSS TOWN.
ZRT
VZTT
VMMMM
I WOULDN'T CALL IT ARMAGEDDON, PER SE. MORE LIKE A NEW BEGINNING.
THE BEAVER OF BONE DESERVES RECOGNITION TOO. NO ONE HAS A DEEPER COMPREHENSION OF MUSIC.
HE'LL CONVERGE THE TONES YOU'RE ABOUT TO EMIT INTO A SINGLE FREQUENCY EASILY--
--TOGETHER, YOU'LL COMPOSE A PITCH SO CATACLYSMIC, SIGHT AND SOUND WILL BE RETURNED TO DUST AND **NOTHINGNESS.**
DOOP
ON
SORRY ABOUT THE SLIGHT ELECTRIC SHOCK. IT WAS A NECESSARY EVIL.

ENGAGE?
YES.
BOMMM
RRAA!
AAAH!
OOOOH!
OOR!
!!
MELODIA
MISTERIUM
ALESEA
ARRRGHHH!
MY EARS!
HURGH!
NO!
OH GOD!
MAKE IT STOP!

ART, YOU'VE GOT TO STOP THIS NOW.
URGH!
AAOW GOD!!
HELLO BROTHER.
AND I SEE YOU'VE BROUGHT THE WHOLE FAMILY WITH YOU. YOU'RE ALL JUST IN TIME FOR THE GRAND FINALE.
NEW
ART, WHAT ARE YOU TRYING TO PROVE? YOU'LL NEVER LEAVE A LEGACY IF THERE'S NO ONE LEFT TO REMEMBER YOU.
OH SPARE ME, KILL.
PUBLIC SPEAKING OBVIOUSLY ISN'T YOUR STRONG SUIT. YOU'RE ABOUT AS CONVINCING AS WRIT.
PLEASE WAKE UP BEAV! EVERYONE'S GOING TO DIE IF YOU DON'T SNAP OUT OF IT!
YOU CAN'T CHANGE DESTINY, LITTLE PILLOW.
YOU'VE BEEN LISTENING IN TO MY REASONS FOR DESTROYING SIGHT AND SOUND. IF THAT'S NOT ENOUGH, WHY SHOULD I BOTHER WASTING MORE BREATH?
I GUESS WORDS WON'T SOLVE THIS...
YEAH, BABY, LET'S DO IT!
NO--
--THIS ONE'S ALL MINE.

WHEN ONE EGG'S HATCHED, ANOTHER ONE'S LAID--
--WHERE DO YOU THINK YOU'RE GOIN' MOTHER CLUCKER?
HUH??
IT LOOKS LIKE YOU'VE SCREWED THIS SITUATION UP.
HEH HEH YEH!
AND ALL THIS TIME I THOUGHT YOU FIXED THINGS.
YEAH, YEAH, GO ON. GO FISHING AROUND IN THAT TRENCH COAT OF YOURS FOR SOMETHING DANGEROUS. CAN'T USE YOUR HANDS LIKE THE REST OF US.
WHAT KIND OF FASHION STATEMENT IS THAT ANYWAYS? ALL IT SAYS TO ME IS "KEEP YOUR CHILDREN AWAY."
POKE FUN GUYS, BUT WHAT'S IN THIS COAT WILL TEACH YOU A VALUABLE LESSON: NEVER BRING FISTS TO A GUN FIGHT.

RRRRR!
!?
CLAP
HOW ABOUT A RIDE? IT'S ON ME.
SLAM!
YOU SEE, KILL...
UGH...
NO ONE GETS IN THE WAY OF MY PLAN. **NOT EVEN FAMILY.**
To Be Continued...

CHAPTER 6

GRAAH!
EVEN IF YOU WON'T DIE--
STUK
--YOU'LL STILL SUFFER.
HRNGH!
WOULDN'T BE THE FIRST TIME.
OOF!

SYSTEM DEACTIVATED.

WHAT THE HELL...

IS IT OVER!?

BEAV?

BEAV!

INITIATING EMERGENCY POWER.

VMM
VMM
VMM
DAMN! I THOUGHT THIS WAS ALL OVER. WE ALREADY STARTED CELEBRATION TIME!
COME ON! DO DO DOOO--
ARGL ARGL ARGL...
NO, NOW IT'S TIME TO SHOW YOU THE GOODS.

THIS IS MORE AWKWARD THAN A CHICKEN WITH A DICK.
IF BY AWKWARD YOU MEAN SLIGHTLY AROUSING.
NEW
!!
OH, HA. HA. HA. IT'S ALL FUN AND GAMES TO YOU, ISN'T IT?
I WONDER WHAT IT'S LIKE TO NOT HAVE A CARE IN THE WORLD.
TSS
GRR!
WHF!
TSS
I GUESS I'LL KNOW SOON ENOUGH. BUT BEFORE THE WORLD ENDS, I'M KILLING SOMEONE.
TSS
NO-
-CHOOCH, FOR SANDERS SAK HELP ME!

DON'T WORRY, CHICKEN. THERE'S SOMETHING FOR EVERYONE IN HERE.
I THINK I'M OK, ACTUALLY...
SQUEE
NEWS
OH GOD.
...BUT WHERE'S THE BATHROOM?
YOU WON'T NEED A BATHROOM WHERE YOU'RE GOING.
HA HA HA HA HA HA
WOOPS!
FSS
AWWWW!
HA HA HA-
FSS S S

AAAAH!
FWOO
AAARGH!
AAH!
YIPE!
EE
WOAH!
SOMEONE GET WATER! HURRY!
ANYONE!
WOO-WOO!
WAY TO BREAK THE SEAL, CHOOCHIE-CHOO!
FWOOO
WHAT?

OH GOD!
FSSSs s s
BEAV, REMEMBER THE BALL? REMEMBER DEEP CUTS? C'MON SNAP OUT OF IT!
SES CAN'T TAKE MUCH MORE DAMAGE, BEAV!
I GUESS THIS IS IT. MAYBE I'LL SEE YOU ON THE OTHER SIDE.
HELP!
PUNT
OP, DROP
ID ROLL!
DEE-- DJ...?
BEAV!
ARE YOU TRYING TO GIVE ME A CONCUSSION, YOU FLUFFY LITTLE BITCH?
YOUR VERBAL ABUSE HAS NEVER MADE ME HAPPIER, BUT WE GOTTA MOVE!
FIRE EXTINGUISHER??? I'M BURNING!

RRRR-
GLAHRK...
SYSTEM DEACTIVATED.
WHAT!?
KAFF!
BROTHER...
GET-UP DAMMIT!
KILL, WATCH OUT!
YOU'VE--
KRUN
--RUINED--

--EVERYTHING!
ART...
SHLOK!
YOUR ACTIONS MUST HAVE IMMEDIATE CONSEQUENCES.
SINCE DEATH ISN'T AN OPTION--
--THIS WILL HAVE TO DO.
YOU ARE SUCH AN ASS.

IF IT WEREN'T FOR YOU AND THAT GROUP OF RETARDS YOU SURROUND YOURSELF WITH, MY PLAN WOULD BE FULLY EXECUTED.
ART, YOU LOST THE MIND OF YOURS.
SHUT THE FUG UP! NOW EVERYONE LISTEN CLOSELY--
--ESPECIALLY YOU.
I COULD REUNITE YOUR FRIEND HERE WITH HIS BODY, BUT YOU CAN BE SURE HE'LL TAKE THE FATHERS STRAIGHT TO CLOCKWORK. MUSIC AS YOU KNOW IT WILL END ALL THE SAME.
DON'T TRY TO MANIPULATE HIM, YOU--
THAT'S ENOUGH OUT OF YOU!
MFF!
DO WHAT'S BEST FOR WHAT YOU LOVE AND GET YOUR ASS BACK IN TH CONDUCTION SEAT.

NO ONE TELLS THE BONE BEAVER WHAT TO DO WITH HIS ASS. IN FACT, I THINK YOU'VE SAID ENOUGH IN GENERAL.
YEAH!
AND SINCE I'M NOT GREAT WITH WORDS MYSELF, THIS WILL HAVE TO DO.
CHUK
SHE COULD TELL RIGHT AWAY, THAT I WAS
BAD TO THE BONE
OH!
WHOD
WHOD
WHUD
HRRNNGH!
LOOKS LIKE ALL THAT FIRE HARD-BOILED MY AMMO.
SCIENCE...
B B BE BAD.
DAMMIT, FIXLER, DEAL WITH THIS MESS!
YOUR BOY COULDN'T TAKE THE HEAT. SO SAY HI FOR ME WHEN YOU'RE GETTING YOUR ASSES RAMMED—
—IN HELL!
AAAR!
B B BAD...
BAD TO THE BONE.
GRR...
B B B BAD...

BAD TO THE BONE
MASTER--KZZT!!
SHK
WAY-TO-TAKE YOUR-TIME. IT'S NOT-LIKE-WE'RE-IN THE-MIDDLE-OF-A CRISIS-OR-ANYTHING.
OW!
COULD YOU COOPERATE FOR ONE DAY WITHOUT ANY LIP?
SPLUTCH
KIDS, BABYSIT YOUR BROTHER. I'D SUGGEST EACH TAKING A HALF--
--HE CAN BE A HANDFUL. DISTRESS, BE A DOLL AND TOSS ME THAT SHIV.
I SHOULD HAVE KILLED YOU WHEN I HAD THE CHANCE!

FWOOP
I DON'T REMEMBER ANY CHANCES.
KAK
OF COURSE THE ONLY OTHER EYEWITNESSES ARE TIED UP.
MAYBE WE SHOULD ASK THEM.
CRUNCH
HACK
DO YOUR THING, PAPAS.
YOU JUST MADE A HUGE MISTAKE.
MURDER.

NO! NO PLEASE!
THIS IS ALL A MISUNDERSTANDING, DEMISE! PLEASE, DON'T LET THEM TAKE ME.
WAIT--WE'RE BROTHERS! I'LL BE TORTURED.
WE MAYBE CAME FROM THE SAME TEST TUBE--
--BUT YOU NO LONGER AR MY BROTHER.
WAIT!
JUST HOLD ON A SECOND.
I KNOW YOU'RE ALL THOROUGHLY PISSED AT ART AND WITH GOOD REASON. HE'LL GET WHAT'S COMING TO HIM FROM CLOCKWORK.

BUT HE'S NOT MY PROBLEM.
EXIT
AHEH-HEM.
ABSOLUTELY BOORISH, DJ.
AWFULLY RUDE TO LEAVE WHILE SOMEONE'S TALKING TO YOU, DON'T YOU THINK SO, BEAV?
EXIT
I WAS SENT HERE TO GET YOU ALL UNDER CONTROL.
AND THAT'S WHAT I'M FINALLY ABOUT TO FUGGIN' DO.
GET THE LEAD OUT, COMPADRES.
IT'S TIME TO FACE THE MUSIC.
KRAKL
NEWS
YOU.ME.CARPARK.NOW

YOU WISH IT WAS THAT EASY.
DON'T YOU SEE, LITTLE MAN?

THERE'S NO CONTROLLING--
--WHAT CAN'T BE STOPPED.

DJ, GET MY BROTHER AND THE GIRLS OUT OF HERE. THE REST OF YOU, COVER MY ASS.
NEWS
BAIL BAIL BA
VOOM
RAAGH
C'MERE, CHOOCH!
KILL! KILL, OH GOD! I THINK I'M SICK!
VERY
WHAT ARE YOU TALKING ABOUT!?
FWEO
OK...
NEWS
SHH...
PROMISE NOT TO TELL?
IT...IT BURNS WHEN I PEE...

DJ, WAIT! WHAT ABOUT, KILL!?
HE'LL BE FINE!
BUT THE OTHERS, THEY--
DISTRESS, I'M SCARED TOO!
BUT THE BEST WE CAN DO IS KEEP OUT OF THEIR WAY.
GO! GO! GO!
UNLESS...
ME TOO!
DAMNIT! WE'RE OUT OF AMMO!
PAMF
RRUGH...
SCORE
ALL OF MY PAPAS, FROM ME TO YOU...
LOAD
POOM
MERRY CRYSTALMETH AND COKE-A-DOODLE DOO!!
ULP

WWWNNNGGUR
NOW, WHILE IT'S DOWN!
BEAV, GIMME A PIECE!
A WHAT!?
PEACHY. A.O.D?
YEAH?
GIMME A LIFT!
HE-CALLED ME-AOD! HE CALLED-ME AOD!
SHING!

SOMETHING I CAN HIT IT WITH!
OH YEAH?
HOW'S THIS?
RRRAA!!
!!

KILL!
BOOM
ARGH!
KRK
DISTRESS, GET OUT OF HERE--
--DON'T WORRY ABOUT ME!
NEVER SEND MEN TO DO A TWO-HEADED FISH WOMAN'S JOB!
READY...
SET...

ARRRR...
RRR...
GET UP, LITTLE MAN. LOOKS LIKE YOU'RE WORKING OVERTIME.

HELP!
THIS SHALL BE YOUR LAST CONCERTO.
ZING
GAH!
THUNK
COMPOSE YOURSELF, BOY!
OW! HEY!
WHAT THE-- CAN'T YOU SHOOT ROCKETS OR SOMETHIN'!!
NEGATIVE.
TH-TOOM
WELL WHAT THE HELL ARE THOSE!?
GLOWSTICKS.
TH-TOOM
AAAAH
C'MON, MAN, DON'T YOU SEE?
REBELLING AGAINST BOUNDARIES IS BETTER THAN BLIND FAITH IN A BROKEN SYSTEM.
I'M JUST DOING MY JOB.

HFF
HFF
HFF
YOU HAVE A MEETING WITH THE BIG MAN.
BUT FIRST, I HAVE SOMETHING TO SETTLE.
COME HERE, BABY. I OWE YOU ONE.
NO, WE'RE EVEN. "TIT FOR TAT" AS COUNTRY SO ELOQUENTLY PUT IT.
UH...
UNF!
COULD SOMEONE GET ME A DAMN STOOL OR SOMETHING?
DON'T WORRY. THIS ONE'S ON ME.

LATER THAT EVENING, WHEN THE DUST HAS SETTLED.
TIK TIK TOK THOK TIK TOK
NONE OF MY WORK COMES WITH A GUARANTEE--
--BUT OBVIOUSLY YOUR BROTHER'S IN NEED OF SOME UPGRADING.
CONTAINMENT
AND A SWIFT KICK IN THE ASS--
--I MEAN THE MAN TRIED TO KICK START ARMAGEDDON.
I TAUGHT YOU NOT TO DWELL ON COULDHAVEBEENS, KILL AUDIO. NATURALLY, I'LL TAKE CARE OF ALL THE DAMAGE CAUSED ON HIS BEHALF.
WHY DON'T WE MOVE ON TO SUCCESS STORIES, LIKE THAT FULL CONTAINMENT UNIT YOU'VE GOT?
HUMOR AN OLD-TIMER WITH THE TALE OF YOUR TRAPPING THE FATHERS. HAPPY ENDINGS ARE SO RARE THESE DAYS.

I GUESS YOU KNEW THEY COULD TURN INTO THAT ROBOT THING?
RATHER CREATIVE, ISN'T IT?

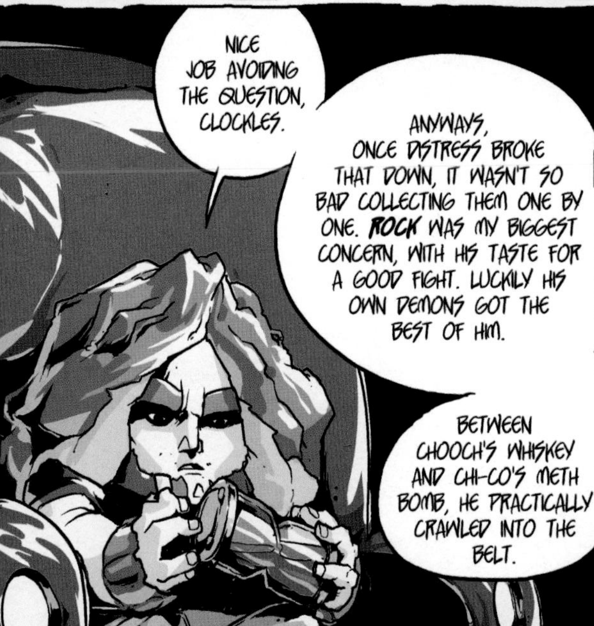
NICE JOB AVOIDING THE QUESTION, CLOCKLES.
ANYWAYS, ONCE DISTRESS BROKE THAT DOWN, IT WASN'T SO BAD COLLECTING THEM ONE BY ONE. ROCK WAS MY BIGGEST CONCERN, WITH HIS TASTE FOR A GOOD FIGHT. LUCKILY HIS OWN DEMONS GOT THE BEST OF HIM.
BETWEEN CHOOCH'S WHISKEY AND CHI-CO'S METH BOMB, HE PRACTICALLY CRAWLED INTO THE BELT.

I JUST WISH WE HADN'T WASTED SO MUCH TIME LOCATING THE FATHERS. GETTING ORGANIZED WAS THREE QUARTERS OF THE BATTLE.
DOK

I TAKE THE BLAME FOR THE LACK OF STRUCTURE. I ADMIT, MY SYSTEM DESIGN WAS FAR TOO DISORGANIZED.

Doop
BUT I CAN ASSURE YOU, THAT'S GOING TO CHANGE. THE FUTURE HOLDS A MUCH SIMPLER LIFE FOR YOU.

YOU'RE STARTING TO SOUND LIKE ONE OF THE CONTROL FREAKS I JUST DEALT WITH...
VRRR

BEHOLD, KILL AUDIO. THE **MILITIA OF VOID**.
I'VE PRODUCED A VOID TO CONTROL **EVERY TYPE** OF IMAGINATION. EVERY SUBGENRE, STYLE OF WRITING, ARTISTIC FUSION--
MIGHT I ALSO BRING UP THE SITUATION WITH ART. IT'S A CLEAR INDICATION THAT THE VOID DOESN'T SEEM TO BE WORKING ALL THAT WELL. BRINGING IN **MILLIONS MORE** OF US MIGHT NOT BE A GREAT IDEA.
VRRR
I SUPPOSE IF YOU CONSIDER AUTHORITY **BORING**.

--EVEN THOSE THAT DON'T EXIST YET.
TICK TOCK TICK TOK
FOR EVERY ACTION, THERE WILL BE AN OFFICER TO APPROVE OR PUNISH IT. AN INFINITE POLICE FORCE OF CREATIVITY.
I MIGHT BE OVERSTEPPING MY BOUNDARIES, BUT IT SOUNDS LIKE YOU'RE CREATING A MATH EQUATION, NOT A BETTER WORLD.
I'M NOT SURE WHAT YOU MEAN.
AREN'T YOU CONCERNED IT'LL BE KIND OF BORING TO LIVE LIKE THAT?
I EXPECTED YOU TO SHOW MORE ENTHUSIASM ABOUT THIS PROMOTION.
WHY CAN'T WE GIVE THE DEMIS A SHOT AT MONITORING THEMSELVES? MAYBE THEY REBEL BECAUSE WE TREAT THEM LIKE CHILDREN WHO CAN'T BE TRUSTED.
I'M GIVING YOU THOUSANDS OF HELPERS TO DO THE DIRTY WORK WHILE YOU RELAX AND OVERSEE IT.
MY APOLOGIES THAT I CAN'T MUSTER UP MORE EXCITEMENT FOR YOUR PLANS TO STERILIZE SIGHT AND SOUND EVEN MORE.
WELL SUIT YOURSELF, BOY. SOME-TIMES PEOPLE DESPISE THEIR OCCUPATIONS. THAT'S WHY IT'S CALLED "WORK."

TIK
TICK
TICK
TIK
Tk
TOCK
YOU KNOW, EVERYONE TALKS ABOUT FINDING A PURPOSE IN THE WORLD. I THOUGHT I FOUND MINE IN **THE VOID**--
--AND EVERY TIME THIS BELT UNRAVELED, IT WAS REASSURANCE THAT MY LIFE WASN'T MEANINGLESS.
NOTHING IN SIGHT AND SOUND IS MEANINGLESS. THAT WOULD BE WASTEFUL.
BUT LOOK AT YOU. THE WORLD IN THE PALM OF YOUR HAND AND YOU DON'T EVEN APPRECIATE IT. WE'RE THE CLOSEST THING YOU HAVE TO FAMILY AND YET, YOU DON'T WANT US TO FIND ANYTHING THAT MAKES US TRULY HAPPY.
ALL YOU CAN THINK ABOUT IS CONTROLLING MORE AND MORE.
I'D RATHER BE INSIGNIFICANT THAN WHAT **YOU** ARE.

I'M THE MASTER OF MY OWN DESTINY AND IF I HAVE TO REMIND YOU, THE MASTER OF ***YOURS.***

NOW GIVE ME ***THE TAPE.***

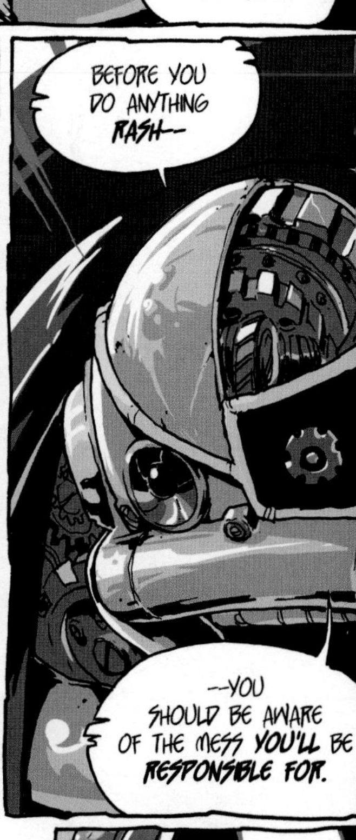

AUUWGH!!
NO!
KILL!
SNRT
I-CAN'T *WHEEEEEEZE* BELIEVE WE'RE BOUND FOR ETERNITY. I'M LIKE A BATTERED SPOUSE.
KILL!!
LUCKILY WE GOT NOTHIN' BUT TIME TO WORK OUT OUR PROBLEMS.
C'MON LET'S GO.

SO, UH, HOW'D IT GO DOWN BABY?
AAAHHH!
AUGH!
WHUMP
WELL...
HE OFFERED ME A RAISE. COMPLETE WITH LESS RESPONSIBILITY, MORE POWER AND A HUGE ENTOURAGE.
AND?
I TOLD HIM I'D RATHER DEEP FRY MY NUTS. PLUS, I ALREADY HAVE ALL THE ENTOURAGE I NEED.
NOW LET'S BLOW THIS HOT DOG STAND.
YOU SHOULD HAVE NEGOTIATED FOR A HAREM, LITTLE MAN. SOME FINE CHICKEN LADIES TO ASSIST THE COKE DADDY.
ASSIST IN WHAT? IT SEEMS TO ME WE'RE UNEMPLOYED, MY FRIENDS.
SO WHAT ARE WE GONNA DO? I DOUBT THEY'LL GIVE ME MY SECURITY JOB BACK HERE AT THE TOWER.
SECURITY? BITCH, YOU WERE A CHEW TOY FOR ROOM AND BOARD!

I VOTE FOR A NICE LONG DETOX, SOMEWHERE RELAXING. HOW DO YOU PEACHES FEEL ABOUT COLOMBIA?
IN UNCERTAIN TIMES LIKE THESE, I ALWAYS SAY THE ONLY THING A MAN CAN BE SURE OF IS THE RIGHT TUNE.
YOU'VE GOT BIG--ALBEIT HORRIFYING-- DREAMS OF RELAXATION, CHI-CO. BUT I CAN'T THINK PAST A DOUBLE SHOT OF WHISKY RIGHT NOW. LET'S START THERE.
AND I CAME PREPARED PLAYAS.
NOW THAT'S A PLAN!
PLAY

RECOMMENDED LISTENING PAGE.

SPIRIT **"TAURUS"**

MILES DAVIS **"BITCHES BREW"**

JUDAS PRIEST **"PAINKILLER"**

JONI MITCHELL **"BIG YELLOW TAXI"**

CHOPIN **"NOCTURNE NO. 19 IN E MINOR"**

CAMP LO **"LUCHINI - THIS IS IT"**

NAT KING COLE **"LET'S FACE THE MUSIC AND DANCE"**

DEAD KENNEDYS **"TOO DRUNK TO F* *K"**

THE JACKSONS **"DESTINY"**

THIN LIZZY **"WHISKEY IN THE JAR"**

QUEEN **"THE SHOW MUST GO ON"**

CON FUNK SHUN **"CHASE ME"**

COVER 1C
MR. SHELDON

XXX

COVER 2A
MR. SHELDON

CHUCKBB

CHUCKBB

OPEN
CLOSED
GO HOME

CHUCKBB

WANTED

COVER 6A
MR. SHELDON

COVER 6B
CHUCK BB

HOT TOPIC COVER ISSUE 6
ALUISIO CERVELLE SANTOS

CHARACTER SKETCHES

JAZZ
VOODOO JAZZ PRIEST
COME INSIDE THE HOO-DOO TRANCE
PIANO KEYS.
WAR
FIXER.
TOOLS INSIDE HIS JACKET.
KNIFE-PARTY.
ROCK'N'ROLL CHOOCHIE CHEW
SOBER & SURLY
Classical
I PRIDE WHAT I DO.
ART MURDER
WRIT END.
YEH?
WOT.
BELT.
BELT
1950's / 18th cent.
STAGE FRONT.
Demise?
Demise O'DRAMA
KA.
PUNK (ish)
PROG
ALL HAT & MOUSTACHE.
COUNTRY
FOLK.
*NOTE: MASSIVE PUBES.

ASK A TOUCAN

Billy "Toucan" Fandango is an ex-street hustler, turned celebrity talk show host and life coach. Do you have a relationship, etiquette or life question? No one has the answers like the Toucan!

Why are there no super heroes in Sight & Sound?
– ladeezundeez202, Alesea, S&S

You might not remember the days when Art Murder was the only gangsta looking after creativity and those dudes in tights were running all over the place tryin' to save the day--butt sweat soaking all up in that spandex. Cleaning up the streets? Shoooot, I say more like stinking it up! Word to the bird is, all them super heroes were let go when Clockwork finished making the rest of the Void. I think S & S is better off—who needs a whole damn city of grape smugglin' fools. You dig?

My friend and I have a disagreement. He says you're unqualified to be giving advice. I say you have many degrees no one knows about. Who's right?
—M.D.maybe, Literialle, S&S

You, my scholarly friend, are correct. I have several. I got a Masters Degree in Kung Fu Ass Kickin', a PhD in Love Bumpin', an MBA in Straight Pimpin'—and a semester of aeronautics. Stay tuned, bee-ytch. This toucan's goin' to deep space.

I bought basketball tickets for my girlfriend. The only problem is I don't have one. You're a ladies man. Can you give me some advice?
—LonesomeDJ, S. Melodia, S&S

Listen, Fluffapotamus: you best get off the bench and start playing. Hit the streets with a box of sweets, ya heard? Ladies love assertion in a pole swingin' Dig Dugger.

Do you think there are other universes out there?
—curiousinmisterium

Sure I do! I believe there's one with 78 planets bound together by some radiant blue sunshine called the Keywork, and some mean monster man's draining the people's life force to keep it goin'...NO, ya dumb ass switch! Of course I don't think there's other universes out there. You on some sci-fi naggle jaggle, so shut it down.

Photo credit: Dave Hamann

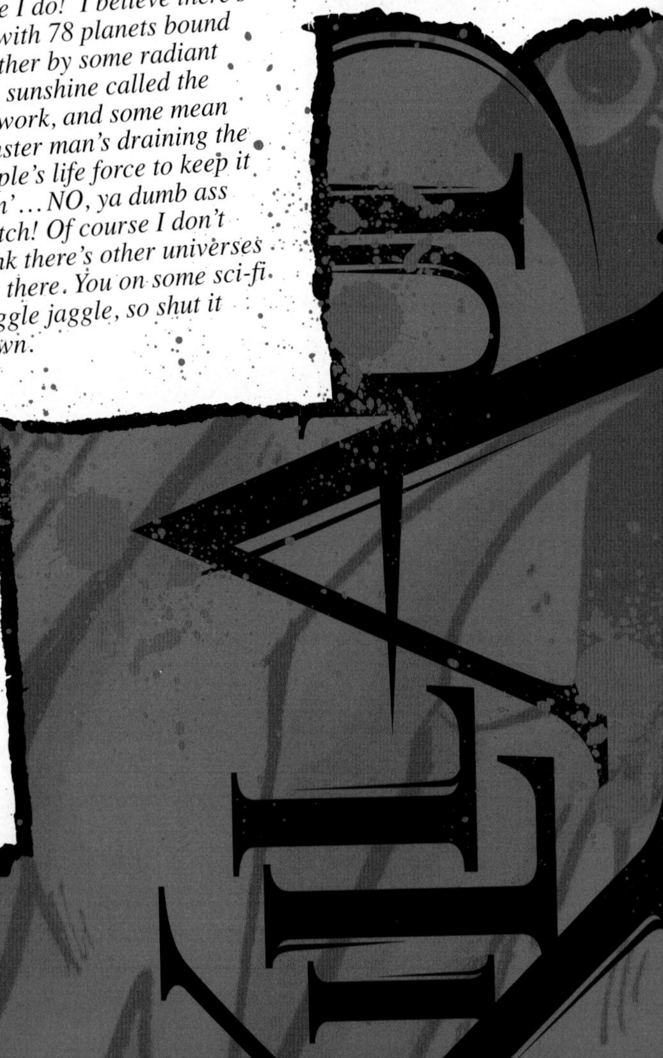

LOVE, CONTRACTUALLY

Story by Claudio Sanchez & Chondra Echert
Written by Chondra Echert
Illustrations by Aluisio Cervelle Santos

It was the young man's first day escorting wide-eyed tourists through the resplendent high-rise offices of LAMP HOLDINGS INTERNATIONAL, in downtown Misterium. As an intern, he'd been fully briefed on the biography of Mr. Lamp, from his decade-long stint as an illustrious superhero to the dates of every major property acquisition that helped elevate him into the position he currently held as the single wealthiest real estate magnate in Sight & Sound. The intern was taught how to seamlessly escort the droves of visitors from the gilded breakroom to the fifty-person conference center, heralded in Business Monthly as the "most extravagant place to hold a meeting to date," where the tourists would *ooh* and *ahhh* over the five dozen endangered elephantiger leather chairs and the massive conference table constructed from 8,000 pounds of pure S & S crystal. To avoid the difficulties of holding onto interns in the past, what the young man hadn't been told about was Mr. Lamp's sometimes unprofessional behavior, that many referred to loosely as "questionable." In social circles, Mr. Lamp was known as an "arrogant prick." It seems the intern would find out for himself, and much sooner than anyone expected him to.

"Behind these doors, ladies and gentlemen, is where the most important deals happen. Mr. Lamp's private office. Note the grain of the exotic wood--"

CRASH!

The enormous doors to the office splayed open, a large potted tree flying through them and spilling dirt across the marble floors. The intern's jaw dropped. The tourists scattered out of the way, snapping photos and peering into the room. The Lamp's brute of a bodyguard and old super hero sidekick, Switch, looked angrily back at them from inside. Behind him, a small creature wearing a black suit and a red cape, his large brain encased in a lamp-like bulb over his head, was standing on a chair, clearly in the middle of a tantrum. His eyes flared out, bulbous and white as he waved a stack of important-looking documents in the face of the man across the desk.

"Do I look like some kind of kid who just got his real estate license and is scrounging around in the cesspools of the inner city projects to afford my average-looking girlfriend's birthday gift, Stewart?"

"No, sir, of course you don't," the man across the desk retorted.

"Then what would possess you to bring these amateur proposals to me and believe I'd have some inkling of interest in remodeling the slums?"

"I thought you might want to take on some more grassroots projects."

"Grassroots is a nice word for poor. I'm far too good at what I do to be bothered with taking on charity cases."

Switch walked towards the door and slammed it in the faces of the captivated rubberneckers, including the intern, who most certainly wouldn't be returning to work tomorrow. Lamp jumped off the chair and walked towards the glass panels that lined the entire left side of his office, running his hand across a glossy photo of himself and Switch, taken during their superhero heydays. He continued.

"In the past, I saved the lives of helpless babies and grandmothers. Now I work 365 days a year. My mind, as you can see, is constantly fixated on the next big venture. How I can be better. Richer.

I surround myself with like-minded people, Stewart, and clearly you are not one of those."

Stewart started to speak, Lamp cutting him off immediately.

"While you've been wasting our time thinking locally, I've been busy developing our company. Expanding to untouched territories. I leave tomorrow for the Mas Grande Ocean. Lamp Holdings has a very secret meeting with Atlaua. I believe it's time we think aquatically."

"Sir, you know there's no way land and sea can merge on the property front. It's in the monopolization clause. Our efforts would be better here," said Stewart.

"Our efforts are no longer relevant. This conversation is over. I'd say we both have some things to pack. Switch, I'll need some business swimwear. Stewart, collect your belongings. You're fired."

***

Two days later, the wheels of Lamp's private jet touched down on the runway at the Mas Grande International Airport after an overnight flight, while five miles below sea level, in the home of the famed Atlaua, the morning was just getting underway. The housekeeper had set the abalone dining table for six and the intoxicating smell of fresh scallop and caviar omelets beckoned the family to wake up.

Atlaua's wife, Aquelle, was the first to rise, elegantly swishing to the bottom level of the home, her robe, made of the finest sea grasses, flowing around her. She was easy on the eyes, with wavy, lavender, waist-length hair and a tail covered entirely in daffodil yellow scales. Still there was a callousness about her that suggested countless years catering to her husband's demanding job as Ruler of the Sea had aged her before her time. Aquelle sat down at the impressive breakfast spread, taking the liberty to pour herself a cup of coral tea so she could effectively take her depression medication. Having grown up in a much shallower part of the Mas Grande, she blamed her inner turmoil on the lack of sunlight so far beneath the sea. But those who knew better attributed the sadness to a combination of boredom, a pessimistic heart and her husband's unmistakable infidelities. That she had the sympathy of the underwater world regarding these affairs did nothing to make her feel better. In fact, Aquelle lashed back at their pity with a cold ambivalence that some mistook for narcissism. She swallowed the large pill in one hot gulp.

A minute or so later, three mermaid girls with matching violet locks came fumbling down the stairs, still in their nightclothes. They were all old enough to move out, get married—at least manage to find a goal or two. But they preferred to lounge around all day and torment their father's assistants instead. They all sat down clumsily at the table.

"I see you started without us, Mother," remarked the eldest of the girls, Marrina. She popped a piece of seaweed in her mouth, a little string of it settling between her front teeth. "That was kind of you."

"You're all too old for formalities. Now quit your blubbering and eat," her mother said, staring off into the distance at nothing.

"Atlaua, are you going to grace us with your presence this morning?" Aquelle bellowed up the stairs.

Coquina, the baby of the family, held her fingers out, inspecting her chipped manicure as she sipped her mug of squid ink. "What's on the agenda today, ladies? I could totally use a mani-pedi if anyone else is interested."

"Can't, I have a date," Oceania said.

"You better seal the deal this time. Could be your only chance to find a man," Marrina cut in, grinning. This was typical banter between the three girls and their mother, a sense of entitlement and sarcasm dripping from every word. Even first thing in the morning.

"You might want to take a look in the mirror at that green crap between your teeth, Swamp Thing. Then you can make fun of others in good conscience," Oceania snapped back. "Mom, what did you have in mind for the day?"

Before she could answer, the great Atlaua appeared, a mass of translucent crimson tentacles moving in time below his torso to carry him across the floor. He was dressed for a day of business—a sun-dried, ray leather structured top that looked like armor with sea urchin skull epaulets at his broad shoulders. As the housekeeper poured him some hot ink, he turned to take it from her, exposing a massive fin that protruded from his lower back, poking out from a glorious tangle of thick transparent hair. Anyone who encountered him was compelled to stop and stare at the majestic ruler of the water worlds, for he was certainly something to behold.

"Good morning, family." He went to each of them, ruffling their hair affectionately. He greeted his wife, moving in for a hello kiss. Aquelle coldly turned her cheek to him. The housekeeper had secretly always wondered whether Atlaua's cheating was the only way he could bear his marriage to a very emotionally unavailable woman or whether it'd made her that way.

"I am going to be in a very important meeting all day," he sipped from the mug, looking at his daughters, "Girls, I want no interruptions from any of you. No traipsing around the boardrooms or tormenting my staff. I have a very special guest coming and must give him my full attention."

Without so much as touching breakfast, Atlaua set the mug down on the table and called to them as he floated out the door, "Enjoy your day. I'll be home for dinner this evening. Don't forget it's Distress's birthday." A convoy of underwater guards waited outside to safely escort him to the biggest meeting that land and sea had ever seen.

The door slammed so loudly, the four women barely noticed a fifth making her way to the table. She was an inky smoke slinking into the room, visually opposite the others. The most obvious difference was that she had not only two heads, both crowned with charcoal black hair, but twin slate colored tails as well. There was nothing dainty about her, but the girl was alluring.

Coquina broke the silence. "Happy birthday, Distress. Wanna get a manicure with me?"

"Thanks, but not today. Morning, everyone," she said, almost under her breath. "Mom."

For the first time all morning, Aquelle looked away from the wall she'd been staring at so intently, focusing in on the girl.

"Distress," she said, "For the last time—I am NOT your mother."

Distress grabbed a seaweed roll from the table and a cup of coral tea as the words cut her. She didn't look back as she went straight back up to her room. By choice, her mouths spoke in union. "I thank god for that everyday."

***

Deep in the heart of the Mas Grande Ocean, Atlaua approached the Foreign Affairs conference building with his entourage of guards, motioning all but two close assistants to remain outside. The place was nothing short of a masterpiece, seashell architecture with cathedral ceilings and stained glass that changed color as the temperature of the water shifted. Inside the meeting room, Lamp had already arrived and was peering out through the watercolor windows, into the abyss of mostly undeveloped sea floor. For the first time in innumerable years, Lamp felt inspired by the possibilities.

Atlaua was announced as he entered the room, each man intrigued to see the other in the flesh. As the two shook hands, Atlaua towered above Lamp, who may have been intimidated save for a serious Napoleon Complex and the loyal Switch by his side, a behemoth of a creature with a portal in his stomach should Lamp need to be transported or protected.

"It is a pleasure to meet you, Mr. Lamp. Word of your valor in fighting crime has reached us here, miles below the water. The only thing more impressive is your success in developing Sight & Sound. You are quite the entrepreneur."

"Thanks for the kindness, Mr. Atlaua. You've been an inspiration to my strategies for a long time, actually. I admire the work you've been doing to cultivate the under water. But truth be told, after taking a look around, I feel you're not taking full advantage of a lot of prime property. I envision a great deal of potential growth, particularly in this city," he motioned outside the glass to the barren space, "**if** I were able to acquire it. That's why I'm here."

Atlaua looked slightly deflated, breathing out massive bubbles as he contemplated what Lamp was saying. "I'm confused, Mr. Lamp. I was under the assumption your visit was as that of a Land Ambassador. You are well-versed on the underwater land ban for foreigners, yes?"

"Very well-versed."

"Then I don't see how we *could* do any real business in that respect. Furthermore, I'm afraid the property you are referring to," Atlaua motioned out the windows, "is reserved strictly for the royal blood line."

"Which is precisely the angle I was hoping you'd see." Lamp's eyes narrowed. "I've heard you have three very lovely daughters. The rumor's been repeated that they don't have much business sense, let alone the ability to successfully develop the prestigious underwater capital."

"My *four* daughters have not shown much interest in land development. But I certainly couldn't force a relationship for capitalist benefits, Mr. Lamp, if that's what you're suggesting."

"Excuse me, but I came here as a favor—to help you turn this wasteland into something great. If you prefer to not leave your legacy, no problem. Lamp Holdings will always have some grand project in the works. But for your own sake and the future of the water world, I think you should take a few days to reconsider. You know where to reach me."

And the two parted ways with a very heavy proposal weighing on their business relationship.

***

Distress had been in her bedroom since the morning's confrontation. Aquelle, in reality, wasn't her mother and that's precisely the reason Distress's birthday was something they'd both dreaded for as long as she could remember. Distress's biological mother was named Lorelae, a flesh and blood Siren, who'd dropped her baby girl off on Atlaua's doorstep the day she was born. In classic Siren form, Lorelae had lured Atlaua in with her intoxicating voice, only, instead of leading him to his death; she'd led him straight to her bedroom. Aquelle knew of the indiscretion even while it was happening, but she hadn't signed up to raise her husband's illegitimate love child. Distress paid for it every day of her life, particularly on this day of the year, when the wound was re-opened for Aquelle.

So she stayed upstairs and worked on a song she'd been writing, playing the chords on a blaring guitar. The girl could sing the blues like no one else.

The notes traveled throughout the house, her voice reverberating through the water and beneath the cracks of each bedroom where the other women had been getting ready for the day. They would never succeed, instead each succumbing to Distress's unintentional Siren song and falling into a deep sleep where they stood. Coquina snored through her manicure, Marrina was silent for once and Oceania slept through what could have been the date of her life. But most unfortunate was Aquelle, who'd been standing at her sea glass vanity applying lipstick when she fell into the trance, dropping to the floor and cutting open her face, from eyebrow to lip, on the jagged countertop. Distress was completely unaware of any of this—until her father walked through the door earlier than expected. As she went down to greet him, a series of shrieks could be heard upstairs. Then, a deep guttural roar. "THAT SEA WITCH HAS DESTROYED MY FACE!"

Atlaua had just walked into a war zone. He looked at Distress who seemed as confused as him, until, Aquelle appeared, her bloody face coloring the water around her as she pressed a cloth to her eye.

"This is it, Distress. It's the last time."

One by one the girls started to awaken, each with their own series of complaints about Distress's song destroying their day before noticing their mother's wounds and hurrying to tend to them. They pushed and prodded at her face while she continued to scream at the stunned Atlaua.

"I've had it with that girl being in our home! Every year is another reminder of you running off with that Siren whore. And on top of it, since she's a deadbeat mom, I've had to deal with all the problems her kid causes. I want Distress OUT, Atlaua." Aquelle was screaming, years of misplaced anger exploding, "*Now*!"

He'd had this conversation too many times and even though Atlaua knew it was horrible, he couldn't help but feel divine intervention at work. Distress ran out the front door, leaving it wide open behind her.

***

When Mr. Lamp and Atlaua met two days later, they still hadn't found her.

"I'm afraid, this union may not be in the cards for us, Mr. Lamp. I had warmed to the idea of my daughter, Distress, being a suitable wife for you, albeit not what you likely had in mind. She's rather obstinate, you see with those two brains of hers and after an argument the other night, she disappeared in a fury," Atlaua said in so soft a tone he was barely audible.

Mr. Lamp struggled to understand. "So what you're telling me is that you were willing to arrange the marriage to this—Distress—only, she ran away?"

"She's old enough that it's no longer running away, I suppose," the Ruler of the Seas said.

"Listen, Altaua, I can take a hint. You want to sit down here with your empty space dreaming up some grand design that will never happen. So you enjoy t—"

"I did truly want this to work, Mr. Lamp. The water world is desperately in need of someone like you, but there's nothing I can do in the little time we have. It's out of my hands." Atlaua appeared truly sad, his tentacles curling inwards below the conference table and that great fin swaying back and forth in the current.

"Well, if anything changes, you have my number. I sincerely hope, for your family's sake, that we're able to work something out one of these days," Mr. Lamp replied, motioning to Switch that it was time to go. The small doors on Switch's abdomen drew open. Mr. Lamp waved his cape, hopped inside and they exited the building to the waiting private sub-jet Mr. Lamp had built specifically for this trip, leaving Atlaua with little hope for the water world.

As the sub-jet took off through the open water, Mr. Lamp and Switch each settled into their own seats, the former sipping a glass of imported bourbon and bitching to whoever would listen about the unsuccessful meeting. He hated not getting his way. Even more so, he hated going back to Sight and Sound empty handed. The craft moved at astronomical speeds, the first of its kind to feature a giant spearhead at the front, reducing water resistance and allowing the jet to simply splice through anything that should not get out of the way quick enough. The sub-jet continued to surge through mountains of glowing red and amethyst coral heads, schools of a million sparkling silver fish darting in all directions.

"The most frustrating part, Snitch, er, Switch," Mr. Lamp showcased the effects of the bourbon, "is that this lil' venture was more like a vacation. And I *hate* vacations." His pupil-less eyes stared out the window, glossing over more than usual. They had entered into a particularly deep part of the Mas Grande, where nearly everything took on a dusky blue tone, like a cerulean camouflage.

"Eh, it's OK, Boss. You tried your damnedest and at the end of the day, you needed a little down time." Switch tried to appease him, in his notoriously sub-harmonic deep tone.

"We should probably go straight to the mountains to draw up some plans. You know that range we acquired behind the Torrent G--**Whatthehellisthat**?? STOP THE PLANE!" Mr. Lamp practically leaped out of his seat.

Switch followed to see what caught him so off guard. Below, a gigantic, navy blue Sea Spider was busy spinning an elaborate web. Those on land had heard of the Sea Spider, but brushed it off as mythological. Seeing it in the flesh for the first time was almost more than they could handle. It was the size of a 3-story building. The plane descended a bit, remaining undetected in the rolling blues as they tried to get a closer look. Mr. Lamp, despite his being drunk, was also the first to notice that the web was not empty. Nestled in the center of the impressive weave, was a girl. Or was it two? He couldn't be sure from this distance, but to avoid having to deal with it, he didn't say anything.

"I could be wrong, but I think that thing is about to eat some innocent mermaids. Boss, we're well-versed in this area. Why don't we go down there and show him how we do things on land," Switch said.

Mr. Lamp was far too out of shape to be fighting crime and to be perfectly frank, he'd also stopped caring about saving lives a long time ago. That's why he'd changed careers. But he couldn't admit it to anyone. Certainly not in a situation where he was on the spot. So he did something about it. Not the something any of them expected, but an action nevertheless.

"Pilot, redirect the jet towards that damn thing and full speed ahead."

"Sir, I don't know if that's the smartest idea. The tip is meant to handle much smaller targets. We could get stuck here for repairs if it's damaged," the pilot reasoned.

"I don't care. Just go for it."

On the ground, the Sea Spider began wrapping its dinner up in webbing, its jagged fangs oozing a yellow pus to aid in digestion as it opened its gaping mouth. There were screams from below as the girls pleaded for the lives. Fortunately for them, the last thing they'd see wasn't destined to be the Sea Spider's tonsils. Instead, they witnessed firsthand, a very expensive sub-jet tearing through the back of the spider's head and out through its mouth. There were bits and pieces of navy brain and that foul yellow pus all over the place. The victims were stunned, even despite the somewhat anti-climactic end to the watery arachnid.

Mr. Lamp was disgusted. "Well there you go, ingestion of the innocent diverted. Now let's just be on our way. How's the engine looking, Captain?"

"Amazingly enough, this thing was more powerful than it looked. We seem to be fine, Sir. You designed one hell of a craft here," said the Pilot.

"Don't you think we should at least get the girls out of there? Drop them off someplace safe? I mean we've gone this far," Switch asked.

Mr. Lamp looked down at the victims through the window. He finally noticed they weren't dealing with an ordinary couple of mermaids—there was only one. With two heads and tails. And a whole heap of dead Sea Spider splattered across all of her parts.

"Ugh. It's some sort of *deformed* creature covered in goo. She'll dirty the jet! If you clean the mess up yourself, fine."

Switch agreed and they loaded the Sea Spider's tasty morsel onto the plane. Mr. Lamp was completely disinterested at first, merely waving in her direction when she came aboard and getting back to the bourbon.

"Thanks for saving me, guys, but I think I could have gotten out myself. I just needed more time, is all, " the girl said, wiping some of the blue skull out of her cleavage.

“Are you insane? You were most certainly not getting out on your own. You should be kissing our feet for killing that thing. What the hell were you doing all the way out here anyways?!” Lamp said, a little more interested in her ambivalence now.

“I was looking for a new place to live. I got into this big fight with my family and…ah, it doesn’t matter. I’m Distress by the way.” She held out her hand to shake Mr. Lamp’s, whose big eyes suddenly lit up, practically to a white flame.

“Distress? As in the daughter of Atlaua?” he asked.

“How do you know my father? I mean, everyone knows of my father, but do you know him personally?”

“You’re about to find out. Switch, get Atlaua. Tell him we’re bringing his little girl home.”

The rest fell haphazardly into place.

** *

Years later, Atlaua stared out the watercolor windows of the Foreign Affairs Conference room, watching the metropolis that had risen up before his eyes. The water world was growing faster than he could account for thanks to his son-in-law. It hadn’t been an easy choice for Atlaua and to this day, though he would deny it, he felt a sense of shame thinking about what had happened.

Atlaua remembered the evening Mr. Lamp had brought Distress home, a mess of Sea Spider and unresolved anger. He proposed the arranged marriage the next day and could almost see the gears of her mind turning when she had to weigh the odds of spending her life with the arrogant prick or the unforgiving step-monster. For Mr. Lamp, the idea of getting two ladies in one was enough to feed his ego and cool any animosity he’d had about marrying the “black sheep” of the daughters. Plus, he’d found himself strangely attracted to Distress’s dauntless spirit—and ultimately her very necessary role in the most prolific business transaction of Lamp Holdings International.

After the wedding, they’d spent the year locally, while Mr. Lamp drew up plans for the city. He gave her an enormous, secluded garden on the outskirts of Sight and Sound—a surprise birthday gift. She was mesmerized by the place. Atlaua took comfort knowing that over the years, Mr. Lamp had fallen madly in love with Distress, to the point of infatuation. And while Distress would never grow to love her husband in a conventional sense, she loved the idea of a happy birthday. Atlaua could live with that.

KILL AUDIO

CLAUDIO SANCHEZ IS THE CO-AUTHOR OF *YEAR OF THE BLACK RAINBOW*, A NOVEL WRITTEN WITH PETER DAVID AS A PREQUEL TO THE HIT COMIC SERIES *THE AMORY WARS: THE SECOND STAGE TURBINE BLADE* AND *IN KEEPING SECRETS OF SILENT EARTH: 3*. HE'S ALSO THE CREATOR OF THE *KEY OF Z* SERIES, *KILL AUDIO*, AND FOUNDER OF EVIL INK COMICS. WHEN HE'S NOT MAKING COMICS, CLAUDIO SINGS AND PLAYS GUITAR IN THE ROCK BAND COHEED & CAMBRIA. HIS WIFE MAKES HIM CRAZY SOMETIMES, BUT HE LOVES IT. (SHHHHH... KEEP IT QUIET. SHE'S RIGHT BELOW!)

CHONDRA ECHERT IS A WRITER, AN AVID LOVER OF GRAPHIC NOVELS, RANCH DRESSING, THE COLOR PINK AND DRIVING HER HUSBAND NUTS. HER WORK HAS BEEN FEATURED MOST RECENTLY IN THE BOOM! STUDIOS COMIC MINISERIES *KEY OF Z* AND *KILL AUDIO*, THE SHORT STORY PROSE ANTHOLOGY *ZOMBIE ST. PETE*, AND *POPGUN 2* FROM IMAGE COMICS. CURRENTLY, SHE SERVES AS CREATIVE CO-DIRECTOR AT EVIL INK COMICS IN NEW YORK, WHILE LONGING FOR THE FLORIDA SUNSHINE.

MR. SHELDON VELLA IS AN AUSTRALIAN-BORN ILLUSTRATOR WITH A LOUD VOICE AND A NICE ARSE. HIS MOST NOTABLE COMIC AFFAIRS INCLUDE *KILL AUDIO*, *SUPERTRON* AND MARVEL'S *DEADPOOL*. HE LOVES MOTÖRHEAD, HIS FAMILY, FRIED CHICKEN, VIDEO-CHAT CONVERSATIONS WITH HIMSELF, AND YOU.

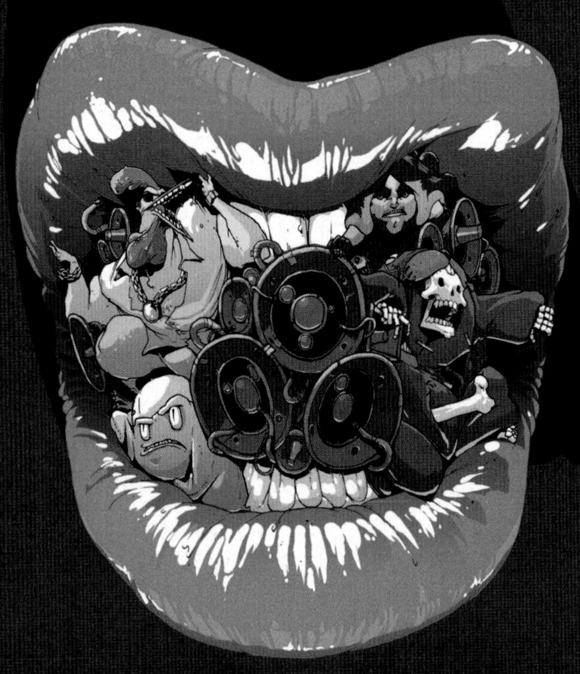